21 Million:
The Bitcoin Paradigm

A Beginner's introduction to the world of Crypto.

SHIN VAYNE

To Satoshi Nakamoto and all Cypherpunks,
who gave me something to write about.

In code we trust!!!

About the Author

My entry into the world of Bitcoin began unexpectedly during my college years. One day, while I was out with my roommate for a smoke, I overheard some of our college seniors talking about some "digital money." I didn't hear all the details, but I recollected hearing the word "bit"—just a small bit of the conversation, but it was enough to ignite my curiosity. What was this new form of money they were talking about?

That moment marked the beginning of my entry into the world of cryptocurrencies. That eager to learn more made me spent countless hours with a sole goal, understand Bitcoin, blockchain technology, and the principles of decentralized finance. With absolutely no formal background in the field, I had to spend countless hours reading whitepapers, joining online crypto forums, and experimenting with various strategies and I was only able to understand a bit of the tech.

In 2020, while the world was in lockdown, I was closely monitoring Bitcoin's market cycles and exploring various theories surrounding its price action and the broader cryptocurrency landscape. This was a time of immense learning, as I dove head first into the patterns of past cycles and studied the underlying economic and technological forces at play. The time at home gave me the opportunity to polish my understanding of crypto and blockchain, and I became addicted to the world of crypto. The way the space was growing and the passion people had, I was slowly and steadily becoming an admirer.

By 2023, I improved my skill set further by learning **Solidity**, the programming language of Ethereum.

As time passed, I started moderating crypto communities. I was talking and chatting with beginners in the space for hours on every day. And now I offer consultancy services for beginners trying to navigate the space.

From overhearing a brief conversation about digital money to becoming a consultant and moderator in the crypto space, my journey has been both challenging and successful. This book is a reflection of that journey—an exploration into Bitcoin and the paradigm shift it represents.

My hope is that it will inspire others to embrace this revolutionary technology and understand how it is reshaping our understanding of money, value, and trust.

Introduction

In a constantly evolving world, few things have remained as essential yet as enigmatic as money. Money is a force that has driven civilizations, toppled empires, and shaped our human destiny in profound ways. Money, at its very core, is much more than the notes and coins in our wallets or the numbers in our bank accounts. It is a concept, a shared belief system that binds societies and fuels economies.

Yet, for all its ubiquity, how often do we stop to ask: *What is money? Where does it come from? And why does it matter?*

In this book we will embark on a journey through the history of money, from its humble beginnings in barter systems to its current form as fiat currency, and beyond. We will explore the economic, social, and technological forces that have shaped money's evolution and enter into the revolutionary idea of Bitcoin—a technology that challenges our fundamental understanding and perceptions about what money can and should be.

Bitcoin is not just a new form of money; it is a new way of thinking about value, trust, and economic freedom. It is gaining momentum at a time when traditional financial systems are under strain, and questions about inflation, centralization, world monetary policies and the very existence of paper money. However, to understand bitcoin one must first understand the very system it seeks to disrupt.

This is why this book starts from the beginning—with the story of money itself. By understanding its history and purpose, we can better appreciate the transformative potential of Bitcoin and our movement towards a decentralized, digital finance. Whether you are an economist, a curious tech nerd, or someone who is eager to understand the buzz around cryptocurrencies, this book aims to provide clarity and context to your curiosity.

In the chapters that follow, you will be navigating through not only the mechanics of blockchain technology but also the deeper implications of a decentralized monetary system. With Bitcoin, we are witnessing the dawn of a new era, an era that promises to reshape our understanding of value and exchange. I hope that this book will not only inform but also inspire you to think critically about the nature of money and the role it plays in our day to day lives.

We will try to go through history, economics and cryptography with examples and analogies. I advise you to read the glossary of terms, if possible, to familiarize with terms.

Welcome to the journey. The future of money awaits.

Chapter-1

Money

Money is one of humanity's most profound inventions. It is so ingrained in our daily lives that we often take its existence for granted. From buying groceries to paying rent, from investing in the stock market to saving for retirement, money is at the heart of nearly every economic activity. But what exactly is money, and how did it come to play such a pivotal role in our lives?

In a simpler context, money is a tool that facilitates trade. In a world without money, people would rely on barter, the direct exchange of goods and services. While barter works in small, simple economies, it quickly becomes inefficient as societies grow. Imagine trying to trade your handmade pottery for a loaf of bread, only to find that the baker doesn't need pottery but would accept apples instead. The absence of a common medium of exchange creates a barrier to trade, limiting economic growth and collaboration.

In a broader context, understanding money is not just an academic exercise; it is essential for navigating the modern world. The decisions we make whether as individuals, businesses, or governments are often influenced by our understanding of money and its value. In an era of rapid technological change and advancements, where digital and decentralized forms of money are becoming increasingly prominent, a solid foundation in the principles of money is more important than ever.

This introduction to money sets the stage for exploring its modern avatars, particularly the advent of Bitcoin and blockchain technology. By understanding the history and purpose of money, we can contemplate and appreciate the revolutionary potential of these innovations. Money related lectures must be promoted from elementary school itself. It is high time and we should help at least the next generation about their understanding of the most important and integral part of human life.

Like any new invention, money also had to go through iterations to suit our vast growing economy and needs. Human beings always found improvements more or less in a trial-and-error method. And we are still developing systems to improve money as we speak. It all started with the limitations with the Barter system.

Barter system had its own short comings. One of the main issues was division of units which was not possible in the barter system. People needed to find others who were willing to exchange goods of the same value. If there's a conflict in the value of the goods, the item in most cases won't be divisible. In simpler terms one cannot trade a part of their horse for an apple.

As societies grew and when the economy demanded more of an efficient system human beings set out for a journey to find an alternate system which would change the course of human history. The humble beginnings of money, and that journey took us from asset backed money to the modern-day inflated currencies.

Now let us address the elephant in the room, Money!! An inflated elephant rather.

Money serves as a universally accepted medium of exchange, solving the inefficiencies of barter. But money is not just a tool for trade. Over time, it has evolved to fulfill three critical functions:

1. **Medium of Exchange:** Money acts as an intermediary in transactions, enabling people to trade goods and services without the complications of barter.

2. **Unit of Account:** It is a standard measure of value, making it easier to compare prices, calculate profits, and understand the relative worth of different items.

3. **Store of Value:** Money preserves purchasing power over time, allowing individuals to save and use for consumption in the future.

Apart from this money should be durable and must withstand repeated use. And if we are on a voyage to find a better system than Barter, we must develop a system which is divisible, easily transported, each unit is identical to the other, and widely recognized and trusted.

We have been mentioning the term alternate systems for quite some time now. But did we find a better system after barter? Hell no!

Throughout history, humanity has sought a better system than barter, but despite our best efforts, we often found ourselves entangled in new challenges. Commodity money, intended to provide stability, led to inequality and scarcity. Fiat money, born from trust in governments, became vulnerable to inflation and manipulation. Even digital money, while offering convenience, introduced concerns over centralization and control.

In search for efficiency, we created systems that failed to meet the promises of fairness and security. It became clear that our solution was merely another iteration of what already existed. And what we needed was a fundamental shift, a new approach to money itself. We will get there eventually, but before that let us brush up on what came after the infamous Barter system.

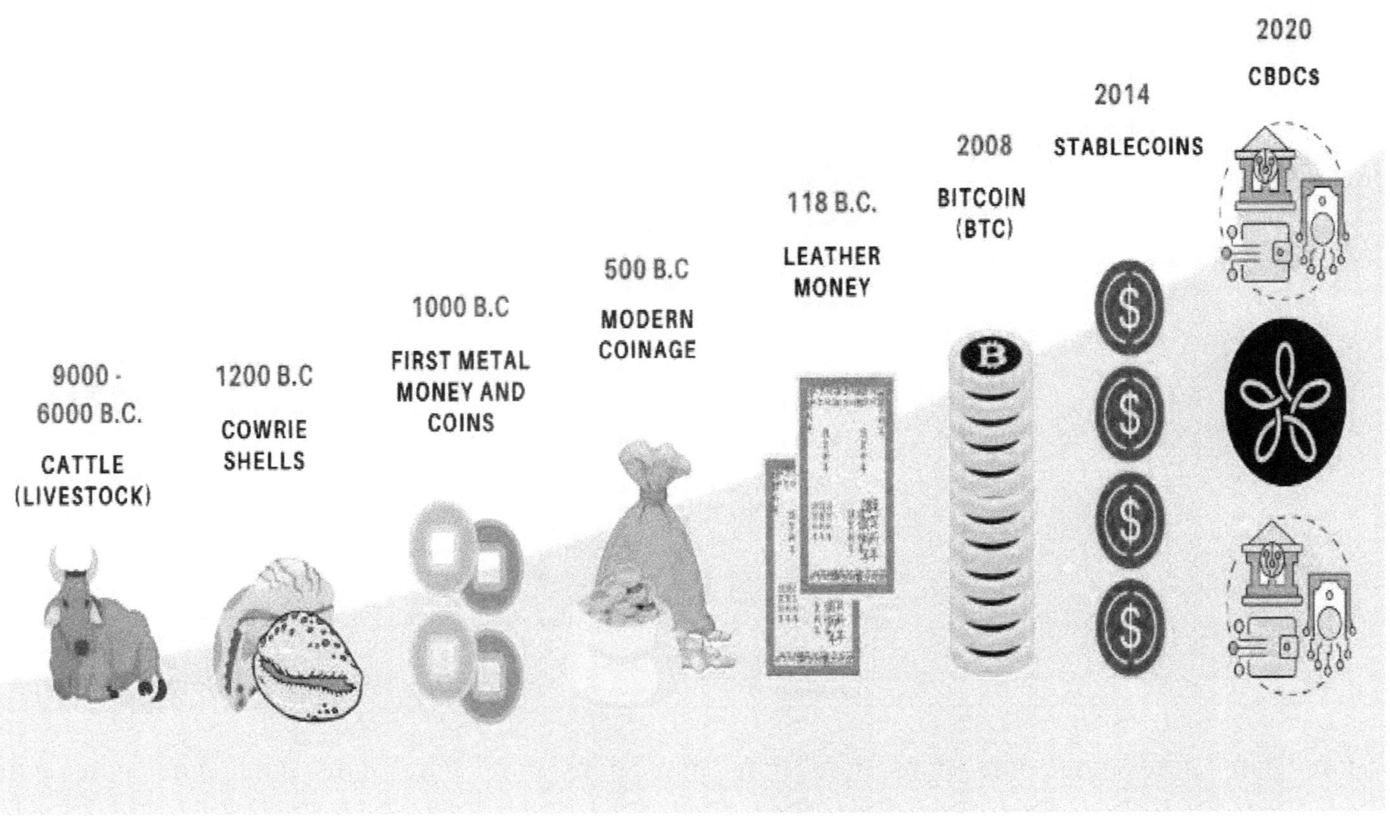

[21Million: The Bitcoin Paradigm]

Chapter -2

Alternate systems

We went through a lot of iterations of money systems. Let's dive into them for a brief amount of time.

Commodity Money

If you were living in that era what would be the first thing you would consider or shortlist as a medium of exchange? Yeah!!! You guessed it right, precious metals!!

If you didn't shame on you 😀

Commodity money is a type of currency where the value comes from the material of the currency itself, rather than an assigned or symbolic worth. Examples include precious metals, agricultural goods, and even unique cultural items like shells or stones.

Gold and silver were the first choice and it had all the ingredients, it is durable, divisible and widely accepted. This was a huge step from the barter system. Commodity money's primary value is in its intrinsic value. This form of money consists of physical items that have a value or utility other than as a form of exchange medium. People would use various goods to buy things and even to satisfy obligations. In that way, the practice of bartering introduced commodity money, in which specific items are given value. That evolved into today's currency systems.

Commodity money included precious metals but was not limited to. Historically, examples of commodity money include **gold, silver, tea, alcohol, and seashells**. Grains, such as barley, were used for trade and commerce during the Mesopotamian civilization around 3000 BC.

A particular quantity of the commodity used for transactions formed a unit of money and units were exchanged based on the perception of the intrinsic value of the item to be purchased. In a way the use of commodity money can still be perceived as barter, but the acceptance of a common denomination by masses that represents a unit of account was a significant transition.

However, these commodities were soon replaced with another form of commodity money, i.e., metal coins, which were primarily made of gold, silver, copper, tin or its alloys. The transition from commodities, like salt, shells and silk, to coins was important because of the inconvenience caused in their transport, storage and the possible perishing and spoilage. Metal coins were much more durable, easy to store and transport than other commodities. These metal coins that acted as denominations were often stamped with pictures and their exchange value was usually controlled by central governing or religious authorities.

The Transition from Commodity Money to Coinage

Early coins were made from precious metals, combining the intrinsic value of commodity money with the convenience of standardization. First coins were said to be minted in the Kingdom of Lydia (circa 600 BCE). Governments began regulating coin production to ensure consistent weight and purity, boosting trust in currency. Moreover, coinage facilitated larger and more complex trade networks by simplifying transactions.

As economies grew, the limitations of finite resources became apparent. The need for a more flexible monetary system led to the adoption of paper money and eventually fiat currency. This was a hybrid system where paper money was backed by gold reserves. It was a compelling alternative but collapsed in the 20th century due to the complexities of maintaining fixed exchange rates.

However, precious metals remain a store of value and hedge against inflation till date. Gold-backed cryptocurrencies, such as PAX Gold, combine the stability of gold with the flexibility of digital currency. Commodities like oil, grain, and metals are now traded as financial instruments, reflecting their enduring economic importance. While some advocate for a return to commodity-backed systems, the limitations in scalability and global trade make such systems impractical.

The intrinsic value of commodities naturally fosters trust, a principle that remains vital in modern monetary systems. Even Bitcoin's fixed supply of 21 million coins mirrors the fixed supply nature of commodities. Although it had its own shortcomings, commodity money demonstrated humanity's ability to iterate monetary systems to suit changing economic and social needs.

Commodity money marked a pivotal role in the evolution of trade and economic systems, and as a system it gave humanity a taste of stability, trust, and universal acceptance. While modern economies moved beyond commodity-based currencies, the ideologies they stood for such as, scarcity, durability, and intrinsic value continue to influence modern financial systems, including cryptocurrencies. This chapter was solely for understanding the history and impact of commodity money which led the way to our modern monetary landscape.

Chapter-3

Fiat money

What drove the evolution of paper money?

Convenience drove the evolution of paper money, when merchants in China as long as 1500 years ago issued promissory notes to avoid using a bulk of metal coins in large commercial transactions with wholesalers. In such cases, the metal coins were left by the merchants with a third party trusted by the transactors and the merchant issued a slip of paper in return for the material obtained from the wholesaler.

The actual coins could later be collected by the wholesaler from the third party entrusted with keeping the coins. Similarly, small pieces of cloth having an exchange rate mentioned on it against silver have been used as a means of trade in Europe as long as 1000 years ago.

But a rapid inflation of precious metals with the exploration of more and more reserves compelled a rethinking regarding how money works. In Europe, gold coins evolved into bank notes in the 17th century, when goldsmith bankers of London started giving out receipts as payable to the bearer of the document irrespective of who was the original depositor. Of course, the goldsmith bankers also realized that they could issue a greater value of bank notes than the physical value of their reserves as not all the notes would be redeemed simultaneously.

A conversion of the large value receipts to multiple smaller fixed denomination receipts for ease of transaction essentially converted these bank notes to currencies with a written order by the goldsmith bankers to pay the amount to whoever was in the possession of the bank note.

Interestingly, issuing bank notes that exceed the value of the precious metal in possession of the bankers leads to a counterparty risk that the bank may not be able to make the payment when presented with the note. The evolution of gold coins into bank notes led to the gold bullion standard in which gold coins no longer circulated in the economy, rather an authority promised to give the bearer of the circulating currency an equivalent amount of gold bullion.

US dollar and the new gold standard

The gold standard is a monetary system in which the value of a country's currency is directly linked to gold. With the gold standard, countries agree to convert paper money into a fixed amount of gold. A country that uses the gold standard sets a price for gold, and it buys and sells gold at that price. The United Kingdom was the first to establish the gold standard.

Bretton Woods agreement.

Approximately 730 delegates representing 44 countries met in Bretton Woods in July 1944 with the principal goals of creating an efficient foreign exchange system, preventing competitive devaluations of currencies, and promoting international economic growth. The Bretton Woods agreement and system played a central role to these goals. The agreement also created two important organizations—the International Monetary Fund (IMF) and the World Bank. Although the Bretton Woods system was dissolved in the 1970s, both the IMF and World Bank have remained strong pillars for the exchange of international currencies.

The purpose of the IMF was to monitor exchange rates and to support nations that needed monetary support. The World Bank, initially called the International Bank for Reconstruction and Development, was established to manage funds available for providing assistance to countries that had been physically and financially affected by World War II. Today, the IMF has 190 member countries and still continues to support global monetary cooperation. In addition, the World Bank provides support through its loans and grants to governments.

Though the Bretton Woods conference itself took place over just three weeks, the planning for it had been going on for several years. The two important figures in the Bretton Woods system were the British economist John Maynard Keynes and chief international economist of the U.S. Treasury Department Harry Dexter White. Keynes' main objective was to create a powerful global central bank called the "Clearing Union" and to issue a new international reserve currency called the bancor. On the other hand, White's plan aimed for a more modest lending fund and a greater role for the U.S. dollar, rather than the creation of a new currency. In the end, the plan came into force took ideas from both, and leaned more toward White's plan.

It wasn't until 1958 that the Bretton Woods system became fully functional. Once implemented, its provisions pointed the U.S. dollar to be pegged to the value of gold. Moreover, all other currencies in the system were then pegged to the U.S. dollar's value. The exchange rate applied at the time set the price of gold at $35 an ounce.

All of the countries in the Bretton Woods system agreed to a fixed peg against the U.S. dollar with diversions of only 1% allowed. All Countries were required to monitor and maintain their currency pegs which they achieved primarily by using their currency to trade U.S. dollars as needed. The Bretton

Woods system, therefore, minimized volatility in international currency exchange rate which boosted international trade relations. The thus achieved stability in foreign currency exchange was also a factor in the successful support of loans and grants internationally from the World Bank.

Long story short, all currencies were pegged to the dollar and dollars were pegged to gold at a price of 35$ for 1 ounce. These enabled countries to use their currencies more efficiently. Indirectly all currencies in this system were backed by gold. But as they say everything good or bad comes to an end eventually. And it did but not in a glamorous way.

Fellow states were concerned about US deficits. France held the baton and started exchanging dollars for gold. The situation became worse when the US went to war in Vietnam. France's concern was every county's concern and in no time, everybody doubted US gold reserves and the amount of dollars in supply.

 When every other member state/country claimed for gold delivery, in 1971 US president Richard Nixon revoked the convertibility of the US dollars for gold. If that was the case then what was pegged to the currencies? Can a country do that? There were a lot of concerns at those times and they did revoke it. From there the term 'fiat currency' came into the picture. If you're here to stay in crypto you will surely hear the term fiat currency every now and then.

Now, what the heck is fiat currency? A fiat system is a monetary system in which the value of a currency is not based on any physical commodity but is instead allowed to fluctuate dynamically against other currencies on the foreign exchange markets. The term "fiat" is derived from the Latin word *fieri*, meaning an arbitrary act or decree.

In keeping with this etymology, the value of fiat currencies is ultimately based on the fact that they are defined as legal tender by way of government decree. This is the economic experiment which caused high levels of inflation we see today. Governments can create money when they desire. That is a lot of power in the hands of law makers and governments. A group of people which fail and rob us in a consistent manner!!

The misuse of power escalated during financial crisis situations. We saw a US bailout of 700 billion dollars during the 2008 financial crisis. And a money printing frenzy during the 2019 COVID pandemic.

Fun fact!! Estimates suggest that approximately 20%-25% of the US dollar was printed in the year 2020. Take a look at the money supply chart.

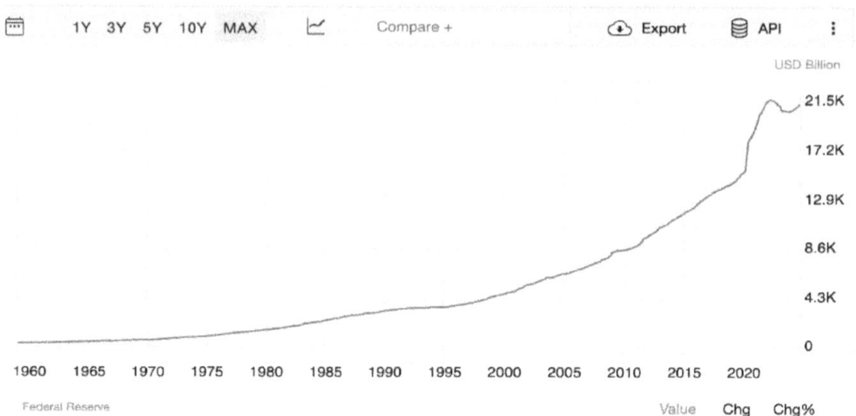

We also have examples of hyperinflation and economic collapses from bad monetary policies. In recent history, the official inflation rate in Zimbabwe averaged 43 percent from 2009 until 2023, reaching up to 786 percent in May 2020. Although these numbers are devastating, but the real hyperinflation happened pre-2009.

The problems in the Zimbabwe economy emerged as early as the 90s due to a wide array of factors including mismanagement, corruption, and the infamous controversial land reform policies. During this time, the Zimbabwean dollar rose rapidly, and inflation peaked at a whopping 79.6 million percent in November of 2008.

Similar was the case in Argentina. Cryptocurrency has exploded in countries like Argentina, where an unstable financial system and strong government intervention in the country's economy has pushed an increasing number of Argentines toward the decentralized nature of bitcoin and cryptocurrencies.

The Argentine peso, the country's national currency, is already highly volatile and subject to a boat load of financial controls that make buying and investing with the currency increasingly unattractive for everyday citizens. Amid this uncertainty however, cryptocurrency has enjoyed a massive boon. According to Chainalysis, Argentines earned $1.86 billion in cryptocurrency in 2021.

Chapter-4

Digital Money

Ahh Money!! The inflated elephant in all its inflationary glory. It is like the air we breathe; it is always around us, sustaining life, shaping the world but hard to pin down. In the current situation money does resemble an inflated balloon which keeps getting bigger and bigger drifting in the blue sky and we cannot overlook the fact that it might pop any second.

We have seen inflation on the rise in most of the places. First with a surge in cost of living and then with supply chain disruptions and shortages in labor. Adding fuel to the fire is the central banks who have been raising interest rates with the aim of cooling things down. But as straight as an arrow we know that this ain't working.

Raising interest rates comes with a bunch of shortcomings, such as slowing growth, increased debt costs, and sometimes even triggering recessions. I have to admit one thing though, 'Recession' is the most used word in YouTube by finfluencers in 2024. So even I might as well throw a bit of recession in there, haha!!

For most of us inflation is like trying to walk on a tightrope. It feels impossible to make both ends meet even though wages are supposed to rise up to loosen that rope. Having said that we don't see wages keeping up and my boy inflation does not even bother waiting for his brother "wages" to keep up, making it a tight squeeze for common people like you and me.

So, in a broader economic perspective inflation is a good old double-edged sword. For debtors like governments and corporations the sword reduces their debt burdens. But for savers, retired folks and anyone with a fixed income it's a nightmare. Tackling money and inflation is like playing competitive sports, we lose our sleep on making money and then lose it again on the decreasing value of the same money we fought hard to make. And beating inflation is the modern-day home run!

So, to put it out here and to put it out here plainly: The value of money is being tested right now. It is like a rollercoaster, hold tight and enjoy but don't be surprised if there's a dip or two. And the major concern unfortunately is are you ready for the ride?

We have a complicated monetary system across the globe. I believe I can call it complicated at the least! And instead of questioning our current system whenever I talk about Bitcoin or crypto to anyone the first question, I usually get is why do we need some digital currency? Don't we have our own legal tender? That is a genuine and a valid question. But before answering that we sure need to find out from where the idea of a digital currency was born.

From whatever we discussed till now I hope that you guys got an idea of our current monetary landscape. We needed a system which supports the common people and not in the hands of governments who can do whatever they wish right? From there the idea of a digital currency were born. The idea of a digital currency was stipulated way before bitcoin came into existence. There were numerous attempts as well to create a currency which was not under the control of governments. Let us list them one by one for your curious mind!! shall we?

eCash – The Birth of Digital Money

eCash was the first attempts to digitize money. It was founded by David Chaum through his company DigiCash. eCash was an anonymous electronic payment system. The core idea was to create an online payment system which was secure, private and as simple as handing over a bank note. To achieve this, it allowed its users to send money online through the internet without relying on traditional banking infrastructure.

To ensure the security and privacy of the transactions, eCash used cryptographic protocols. The system had a provision called 'Digital coin' which could be spent only once and then destroyed after use, mimicking the way physical cash operates. This was the first implementation of a digital currency and it laid the groundwork for later tech like zero knowledge proofs and public-key cryptography which are the pillars of modern-day cryptocurrencies.

Unfortunately, despite its ground breaking ideology and innovative nature eCash faced several obstacles. It struggled to gain traction with users and businesses, partly because it demanded users to open accounts at specific banks and run proprietary software. After we add the regulatory challenges it faced and the failure of mass adoption, the collapse of DigiCash occurred in the late 1990s.

eGold: The Digital Gold Standard

In 1990s, the digital landscape was ripe enough for innovations in new forms of money. During those times

Douglas Jackson and Barry Downey entered the digital money space with a new currency platform; enter eGold!

eGold allowed its users to hold, transfer and store gold online. Yeah, you heard it right Gold!!! This was achieved by effectively creating a form of digital money which was backed by real world assets. Unlike eCash, which was using digital coins, eGold went for a conventional and traditional approach and modernized it to be digital.

A user must create an account with the system to use eGold. Users use this account to store and transfer gold grams. One gram of gold was represented by specific unit of eGold. eGold gained traction rapidly, especially during the early 2000s.While it was a clever way to digitize gold the system faced numerous hurdles. Its centralized nature was pleading intervention from governments.

And in the mid-2000s they got what they pleaded for. The US government seized eGold's assets and accused them for charges like money laundering and other illegal activities. Typical USA!! And finally, the day came and it shut down in 2009.

bMoney

Cryptographer Wei Dai in 1998 proposed bMoney, a system that first introduced some of the key ideas which were later used in Bitcoin. Unlike previous attempts bMoney stressed on decentralization, that is without a central authority or intermediary. bMoney was never implemented but it served as a theoretical model for future decentralized financial systems.

The core of bMoney was the creation of money in a system and transacting it through the same system in a decentralized manner. bMoney also talked about distributed ledgers where all transaction validation was done by users. This is way similar to the modern day blockchain systems. It also stated that digital signature and cryptographic protocols will be used to verify the authenticity of the transactions and the users will work together to avoid and prevent double spending.

bMoney was never implemented due to restriction in technology at that time. At the time, cryptographic technology and protocols required for such a decentralize system was not developed and there was no scalable network infrastructure to support it.

Despite its lack of implementation, bMoney paved ways for the creation of bitcoin. It was one of the first proposals which influenced the creation of a system like bitcoin by laying the groundwork for the development of tech like blockchain and decentralized financial systems.

Fun fact!!! Satoshi referenced bMoney in the Bitcoin whitepaper. The influence it has on Bitcoin is undeniable.

Nick Szabo and the Idea of Bit Gold

Nick Szabo, a computer scientist, a legal scholar and a cryptographer is one of the most influential figures in the development of Bitcoin. He proposed the idea of Bit Gold in 1998. Bit Gold was Szabo's implementation of a decentralized digital currency. It would work similar to gold but without central authorities.

BitGold would create a system where participants will mine gold like tokens (or 'bits') by solving cryptographic puzzles. These tokens will be the currency of the network and will be transacted by the users. The process of mining will be based on the proof of work mechanism, much like Bitcoin. His vision was a distributed network where trust was built through computational effort rather than the reliance on a central authority

Although the concept was brilliant, the infrastructure and tech required was not feasible at that time. Moreover, the idea lacked a secure method in which computational proof can be linked to a monetary value in a way which could be trusted by all parties involved.

Till date Bit Gold is considered as a precursor to Bitcoin. All concepts of Szabo were later implemented in Bitcoin by Satoshi Nakamoto. Additionally, Szabo's idea of smart contracts was implemented by Vitalik Buterin in Ethereum. Gosh!! Szabo was the real deal, a true visionary.

HashCash

While eCash, eGold and Bit Gold aimed to create a new digital currency, HashCash has other ideas in mind and took a more different approach. Introduced by the legendary Adam back in 1997 it was developed to solve completely another problem- email spam. Yeah, you heard it right! Hashcash was a proof of work system which required users to solve cryptographic puzzles before sending an email. This prevented spammers from flooding your inbox.

The senders are required to include a computational proof called a 'Hash' as a part of the email header. This proved that the sender had done a certain amount of effort, making it time consuming and costly for spammers. Especially for large emails. Although the idea was to prevent spam the underlying proof of work was later used in Bitcoin to validate blocks. We will talk about proof of work in detail later. Don't worry!

It was a well thought system but did not gain transaction for deterring email spam. But who knew it would lay the groundwork for Bitcoin in the future. It became the bedrock of the bitcoin consensus mechanism which secures the Bitcoin network.

Bitcoin thus became the direct descendant of Adam Back's HashCash and its role in Bitcoin's success cannot be overstated.

Despite the numerous attempts, we had to wait till 2008 to get what we deserved in the first place!!!

Chapter -5

Bitcoin a peer-to-peer currency network

In a website named bitcoin.org amidst the 2008 financial crisis a whitepaper emerged, claiming that it was decentralized peer to peer currency secured by cryptography. The name of the system was Bitcoin and was published under a pseudonym Satoshi Nakamoto. The whitepaper outlined the core principles of the decentralized currency. The whitepaper described how Bitcoin uses a groundbreaking technology called blockchain to ensure transparency, security, and decentralization.

Bitcoin: A Peer-to-Peer Electronic Cash System

Satoshi Nakamoto
satoshin@gmx.com
www.bitcoin.org

Abstract. A purely peer-to-peer version of electronic cash would allow online payments to be sent directly from one party to another without going through a financial institution. Digital signatures provide part of the solution, but the main benefits are lost if a trusted third party is still required to prevent double-spending. We propose a solution to the double-spending problem using a peer-to-peer network. The network timestamps transactions by hashing them into an ongoing chain of hash-based proof-of-work, forming a record that cannot be changed without redoing the proof-of-work. The longest chain not only serves as proof of the sequence of events witnessed, but proof that it came from the largest pool of CPU power. As long as a majority of CPU power is controlled by nodes that are not cooperating to attack the network, they'll generate the longest chain and outpace attackers. The network itself requires minimal structure. Messages are broadcast on a best effort basis, and nodes can leave and rejoin the network at will, accepting the longest proof-of-work chain as proof of what happened while they were gone.

The whitepaper was simple but had a detailed description of the underlying tech. Bitcoin is a mixture of technology bundled into a serious package. Main tech involved in bitcoin are as follows

-Blockchain

-Distributed Ledger Technology

-Proof of work

-Elliptical curve Digital Signature Algorithm (ECDSA 256)

-Secure Hash Algorithm 256(SHA 256)

<u>-Nakamoto Consensus</u>

<u>-Unspent Transaction Output</u>

<u>-Bitcoin Script</u>

We will cover the above-mentioned topics one by one.

 We already talked about the qualities of money. Does bitcoin have them too? Short answer is yes of course. It is durable and divisible. One quality we are on our way too is its wide acceptance.

Before diving into the tech let us have a brief history lesson on bitcoin and some fun facts.

Some Fun Facts!!!

Satoshi Nakamoto single handedly did not create bitcoin. He was talking to cypherpunks through a mailing list. Names on the list were all pioneers in the world of computer science and cryptography. Such as Adam back (Dev of Hashcash), Nick Szabo (Smart contracts), Hal Finney (Developed Proof of work) and so on and so forth.

Satoshi was active on bitcoin talk forum explaining bitcoin to everyone. You can trace his original messages from the bitcoin forum. So, all bright minded cryptographers were all working for a common goal 'Bitcoin'!

Satoshi Nakamoto's whereabouts is still a mystery and we definitely have no idea whether the founder is male, female, a group of people or even the US government for that matter.

Satoshi did mine the first few blocks and his wallet has close to a million bitcoin which is untouched till date. At the time of writing, at an effective price or 96,000$ per bitcoin his stash is worth 106 billion dollars making him the 14th richest man on planet earth. Damn!! That's a lot of money!!

The first block was called the "Genesis Block" or Block 0 and was mined on Jan 03 2009 which had the now famous message "The times 03/Jan/2009Chancelor on the brink of second bailout for banks"

Key Milestones in Bitcoin's History

2009

-On January 12 2009, the first transaction on the bitcoin blockchain took place. Satoshi sent the first Tx to Hal Finney a developer and early Bitcoin enthusiast. In that Tx Finney received 10 BTC, marking the beginning of the Bitcoin revolution.

2010

-The first real world purchase using bitcoin took place in May 22 2010 when a programmer named Laszlo Hanyecz purchased two pizzas for 10,000 BTC. This day is the now celebrated infamous "Bitcoin pizza day"

2011

-Bitcoin kissed dollar parity for the first time in 2011, trading at a modest 1$ per BTC. Seems silly toady but this was a major milestone for bitcoin and increased attention from fintech communities.

2013

-Bitcoin rallied to 1000$ and crossed it for the first time. This growth was primarily from the growing investor count and the introduction of a new bitcoin exchange called Mt. Gox. However, Mt. Gox collapsed in 2014 due to mismanagement and hacks.

2017

In December of 2017 Bitcoin touched an all-time high of 20,000$ and captured the long-time coming media attention. This also marked the new era in crypto markets and paved way for alternate coins.

2020-2021

Major companies like MicroStrategy, Tesla and Square added Bitcoin to their balance sheets. El Salvador accepted Bitcoin as their legal tender and became the first country to do so.

2024

Bitcoin touched the 100,000$ mark in 2024 Q4 and the asset is now considered by giants like BlackRock, Vanguard etc. 2024 was also the year of Bitcoin ETFs.

Bitcoin achieved quiet a lot in just fifteen years but it wasn't smooth sailing throughout. Bitcoin had to be in the war front for a long time. Faced scrutiny from governments since its inception. Governments have tried everything; they tried banning bitcoin first, when they failed thought about regulating it. When some governments resisted some embraced the tech. Anybody who feared bitcoin waged war against it. The energy intensive mining process also were criticized globally.

Bitcoin's journey has just begun and has a long route ahead. It will be questioned and scrutinized. Will it be the reserve currency? Will it be a store of value? Will it be digital gold? Who knows. Regardless of its trajectory Bitcoin sure did leave a permanent mark on the financial world. Bitcoin inspired a new era of decentralized finance.

The journey of Bitcoin is a true testament to the power of ideas to enter and disrupt well followed and maintained systems. And it wasn't just an idea put into action; it was a movement.

Chapter-6

Blockchain

We needed a revolutionary tech to underpin Bitcoin and Satoshi opted for Blockchain technology. In the flesh, a blockchain is an immutable decentralized ledger which allows its users to carry out peer to peer transactions without a third party.

Although, blockchain found its way beyond Bitcoin too, including financial applications, supply chain management and to identity management. This chapter however emphasizes on the fundamental and core concepts of the Bitcoin Blockchain, its key components, and address the fact that why it serves as the cornerstone for Bitcoin's success.

So long story short, we needed a cradle for our baby and the best cradle we could find at the time was blockchain. Yeah, I know! what the heck is Blockchain right? Let us find out, shall we?

I hope you guys remember a hardcover book which were used in banks and normal shops to keep track of transactions. Yep! I am talking about a 'Ledger'.

Whomever keeping a record of transactions fills the ledger page by page. Similar to a physical ledger think about a digital ledger. Here instead of the whole ledger let us consider page by page.

Like a physical paper this digital ledger also has a limit. In a physical paper it's the number of lines on that page, here it is mentioned as size or number of transactions. Once the page is filled, we turn the page and move on to the next. Here, imagine as if instead of turning the page we tear it and lock the page inside a cube under lock and key. This cube is called a 'BLOCK'.

To keep track of old transactions and for reference we keep the ledgers safely. Similarly, once the succeeding digital ledgers are filled, we get a new cube and we connect it to the old cube to go back and refer to old transactions. So, with each page comes a new cube and all the cubes are interconnected.

For easier understanding imagine the blocks are inter connected using chains similar to a train with multiple compartments. From the explanation is how the name came into existence. A number of blocks connected as a chain; 'Blockchain. Blocks connected as a chain; Blockchain.

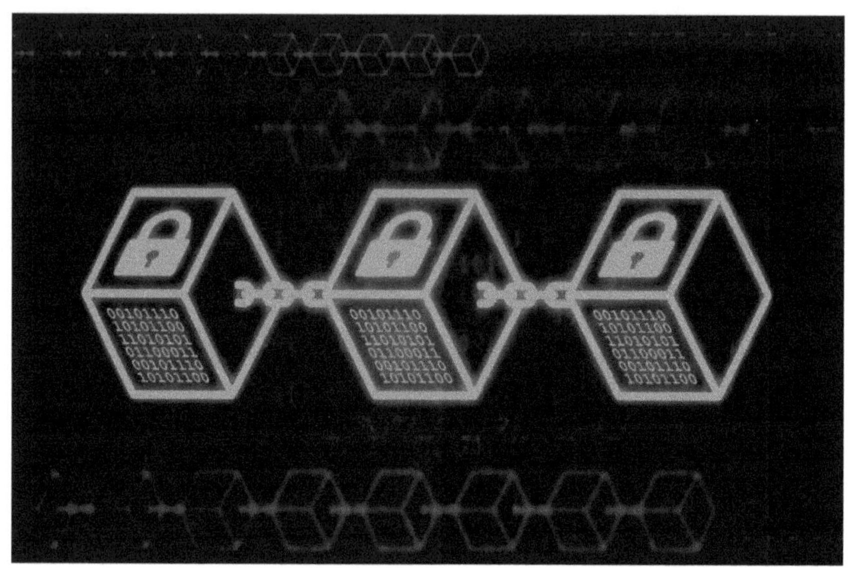

Satoshi never mentioned anything about the term 'Blockchain' he called it 'Timestamp server'. This is a simpler examination to make you understand the basics of the tech involved. Now let us deep dive into the tech.

What is a blockchain?

At its heart, a blockchain as we said is a chain of blocks which contain a number of transactions. Each block is linked to the previous block using cryptographic hashes thus achieving immutability.

A blockchain is designed to be decentralized, immutable and transparent. In simple words, no single authority controls the network, once a data is recorded it cannot be altered without consensus, and all participants can verify the data on chain at any time.

As any technology Blockchain too has its own integral components. They are:

a. Blocks

Block is similar to the foundation of a building. It is the fundamental unit of a blockchain. Each Block contains **Data, Hash and Previous Block Hash**

- Data is the information about the transactions, smart contracts or any other records.
- A unique identifier of the block called a Hash
- A link to previous block called the previous block hash.

b. Nodes

Nodes are the computers in the network who stores the exact copy of the blockchain and validate new transactions. Nodes ensures the security and decentralization of a blockchain.

c.Cryptography

Blockchain is secured by cryptographic algorithms

- Hashing (SHA 256 in Bitcoin) ensures the integrity of the Bitcoin Blockchain.
- Public key Cryptography which secures the transaction by creating unique digital signatures.

We will surely discuss the above-mentioned topics in detail in the following chapters.

In Bitcoin, blockchain is used to maintain a ledger of transactions. The key components of block chain align perfectly with the ideologies of Bitcoin; decentralization, security and transparency.

Although the idea of Blockchain was stipulated in the 1990s the robustness of the tech attracted attention from various sectors till date. A few of them are:

- **Finance sector**- Blockchain power decentralized finance (DeFi) platforms for lending, borrowing and trading.
- **Supply chain**: Blockchain provides transparency and traceability for goods and products.

- **Healthcare**: Blockchain can securely store patient data without leaks thus ensuring privacy.

- **Identity Management**: Any digital identity created or maintained on a blockchain is secure, verifiable and cannot be duplicated.

Chapter-7

Distributed Ledger Technology (DLT)

One of the main hurdles a digital currency should overcome is a 'Double spend attack'. Yeah!! Yeah!! I know, What the heck is double spend attack right?

Good question! Let us take an example.

I borrowed 1000$ from you a few months back and now I have 1000$ in my account and I am ready to pay back the debt. I ask for your credential's blah! Blah! Blah! And I sent you the money. After the transaction let us say I fooled or hacked the bank server and told the server that my balance is still 1000$ and I bought a brand-new iPhone with that fake transaction. So here I spent my 1000$ to clear your debt and bought an iPhone. I spent the 1000$ twice or in better words I double spent the same amount.

So double-spending is a problem that arises when transacting digital currency that involves the same tender being spent multiple times. Multiple transactions sharing the same input broadcasted on the network can be problematic and is a flaw unique to digital currencies. The primary reason for double-spending is that digital currency can be very easily reproduced.

And we need to prevent this from happening. Satoshi was a clever man like me so he thought about it. That's where DLT comes into the picture. DLT serves as the broader category within which blockchain exists, and its principles have given rise to a range of applications beyond cryptocurrencies. This chapter is to understand the concept of DLT, its architecture, key features, and its role in Bitcoin.

Distributed Ledger Technology (DLT) plays a major role in Bitcoin behind the scene and in many other decentralized systems and as the name suggests we distribute the ledger across the network. But to whom?

Every computer on the bitcoin network is called a 'Node'. The moment the ledger is filled and locked in a block a copy of this ledger is sent to all the nodes. Each and every node keeps the whole copy of the blockchain in their computers. As of December 2024, the whole bitcoin blockchain has a size of 685GB. Which means a node has 685Gb of transaction data in his/her computer.

So long story short DLT refers to a digital system for recording transactions across multiple locations simultaneously, eliminating the need for a central authority.

This is important because the nodes are like witnesses to a murder. They can be called up anytime to ask about the crime details. Here we use the witnesses to prevent the good old double spending.

Now think about a bad actor executing a double spend. The computer filling the ledger will ask the whole network about the transaction. Every node replies back after referring to their copy and catches him red handedly and prevents him from double spending. Bitcoin has other ways to prevent double spend as well but that is a story for a future chapter. Sit tight!!

DLT keeps the network together. Even when a part of the network is under attack the network as a whole remains intact because there is no central point of failure. DLT also fosters trust as the ledger is transparent and can be viewed at your will any time.

Having said that DLT comes with its own set of drawbacks: DLT is implemented in Bitcoin in such a way that one block is created every 10 mins. This is to ensure that the copies are validated by as many nodes as possible. But the caveat here is that Bitcoin can only process 7 Tx per second. That is considered slow in today's standards. An array of updates has been done on bitcoin to scale the chain. Keep the updates aside for now and keep in mind that bitcoin is slow, For now!

But why can't we increase the through put right? We have an issue. It cannot be done on the main chain due to a theory called the "Blockchain Trilemma". A triangle love story!!!

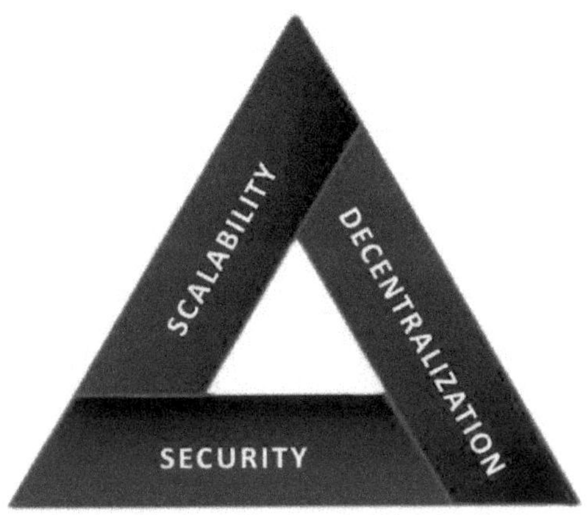

The three individuals in love are scalability, decentralization and security. This theory was put forward by Vitalik Buterin, the founder of Ethereum. It states that out of the three components only two can be achieved. So, if we increase the number of Tx on the bitcoin blockchain or in other words if we scale the chain we sacrifice security. Why?

Because faster transactions mean not enough number of node validations. Lesser nodes mean less witnesses. Fortunately, there are work arounds to this and Bitcoin upgrades are for that. We will talk about all the upgrades don't worry.

Bitcoin is considered slow by people who compare bitcoin to providers like visa with a throughput of 1700 Tx per second. But visa is the fifth or so layer above the base money settlement channels. And although card payments seem instant, the actual settlement between provider and banks may take up to 90 days. On the other hand, Bitcoin Tx once verified are settled.

So, moral of the story is to keep this network safe we need nodes. More nodes mean more copies and more copies means more secure the blockchain is. However, to obtain this security each node should run the bitcoin client software 24/7 which eats electricity. Then why should they do it? I am an Indian, I would not do anything if I didn't get paid. As far as now bitcoin looks similar to a bank with employees called nodes. Bank staff get paid. What about our staff?

Chapter-8

Consensus and Reward

Decentralized systems lack a central authority to validate and secure transactions. Without consensus, the network would be vulnerable to attacks, fraud, and inconsistencies. Moreover, all honest participants must agree on the validity of transactions. And all participants should have the opportunity to contribute to the consensus process as well. And most importantly once consensus is achieved, the decision must be final and cannot be easily reversed.

But what the heck is consensus!! Let us understand consensus using our traditional bank accounts.

How and what all is required for a transaction to occur in traditional banking?

- Both parties need a bank account.
- One or more banks if both have accounts with different banks.
- Sender should have the required amount in his bank account

- Most importantly if the bank feels there is any security issue, they will not let you make the transaction

Here a whole bunch of factors such as bank staff, servers and individuals should agree on everything unanimously for a Tx to occur. This is called Consensus. In other words, a unanimous agreement for a common goal.

Consensus mechanisms are the backbone of any decentralized system, enabling a network of participants to agree on the validity of transactions without relying on a central authority. These mechanisms are critical for maintaining the integrity, security, and functionality of distributed ledgers, such as blockchain. But as we said earlier bank staff do get paid. We need to incentivize people on the bitcoin network as well.

So how does bitcoin incentivize their staff?

Once a computer fills a ledger and creates a block, that particular computer can add one more transaction to the ledger. This transaction in particular will have that person's wallet address claiming for a payment for the work he has done.

We cannot pay in fiat currency, right? That would fail the sole purpose for which bitcoin was created in the first place.

Instead of that the block creator gets the reward in bitcoins. This is called 'Block Reward'.

In 2009 when the protocol kickstarted the block reward was 50 BTC per block. That means a computer who creates a block will receive 50 BTC as reward. This is the only way bitcoin comes into existence. Nobody else can create bitcoin other than the block creators.

Sounds good in today's terms, right? 50 BTC is worth 5,000,000 right now!

But this poses a serious issue. On an average it takes around 10 mins to create one block on the Bitcoin blockchain. That means every 10 mins 50BTC comes into existence. If you do the math, it will be 300 BTC in an hour and 7200 BTC in one day. This means bitcoin will forever print money at a rate of 7200 units per day.

Congratulations!! We have created yet another fiat printer!! But! Satoshi, being a clever man as usual, avoided this big mistake.To prevent this once every 210,000 blocks the block reward is cut into half. This is called the infamous 'Bitcoin Halving'.10 min block time means this usually takes around 4 years. We have had four halving events since the inception of BTC.

- Nov. 28, 2012, to 25 bitcoins
- July 9, 2016, to 12.5 bitcoins
- May 11, 2020, to 6.25 bitcoins
- April 19, 2024, to 3.125 bitcoins

So now if someone creates a block, he will receive 3.125 BTC as block reward. Let us put this into supply perspective. In the beginning we said bitcoin was divisible as money. Most of our currency has two decimals. That is 1 dollar is 1.00$. But bitcoin can be divided to 100 millionth of one unit. In simple words it has 8 decimal points. These units are referred to as 'satoshis' or 'Sats' like cents to the dollar.

So, we can half it till 0.00000001. If you do the cumbersome math the last bitcoin will be mined by 2140 and there will be 21 million BTC in the whole world. This is how that magical 21 million number comes into the picture. Now we have an asset with a supply cap of 21 million units. This fixed supply gives Bitcoin the name 'Digital Gold'.

A pictorial interpretation is given in the next page. This process where computers create bitcoin is referred to as 'Mining' similar to gold mining. Here you mine from blocks instead of mining from the ground.

Halving Events (Est.)	Block Number	Block Reward	Circulating Bitcoin Supply
2009	0	50	10,5000,000
2012	210,000	25	15,750,000
2016	420,000	12.5	18,375,000
2020	630,000	6.25	19,687,500
2024	840,000	3.125	20,343,750
2028	1,050,000	1.5625	20,671,875
2032	1,260,000	0.78125	20,835,937.5
2036	1,470,000	0.390625	20,917,968.75
2040	1,680,000	0.19531250	20,958,984.375
2044	1,890,000	0.09765625	20,979,492.1875
2048	2,100,000	0.04882812	20,989,746.0927
2052	2,310,000	0.02441406	20,994,873.0453
2056	2,520,000	0.01220703	20,997,436.5216
2060	2,730,000	0.00610351	20,998,718.2587
2064	2,940,000	0.00305175	20,999,359.1262
2068	3,150,000	0.00152587	20,999,679.5589
2072	3,360,000	0.00076293	20,999,839.7742
2076	3,570,000	0.00038146	20,999,919.8808
2080	3,780,000	0.00019073	20,999,959.9341
2084	3,990,000	0.00009536	20,999,979.9597
2088	4,200,000	0.00004768	20,999,989.9725
2092	4,410,000	0.00002384	20,999,994.9789
2096	4,620,000	0.00001192	20,999,997.4821
2100	4,830,000	0.00000596	20,999,998.7337
2104	5,040,000	0.00000298	20,999,999.3595
2108	5,250,000	0.00000149	20,999,999.6724
2112	5,460,000	0.00000074	20,999,999.8278
2116	5,670,000	0.00000037	20,999,999.9055
2120	5,880,000	0.00000018	20,999,999.9433
2124	6,090,000	0.00000009	20,999,999.9622
2128	6,300,000	0.00000004	20,999,999.9706
2132	6,510,000	0.00000002	20,999,999.9748
2136	6,720,000	0.00000001	20,999,999.9769
2140	6,930,000	0.00000000	20,999,999.9769

Chapter-9

Secure Hash Algorithm 256 (SHA-256)

Bitcoin comes from block rewards. We need to secure the blocks as foolproof as possible. Satoshi chose SHA 256 to do that. Secure Hash Algorithm was developed by none other than the National Security Agency (NSA) of USA and was released in the year 2001. SHA is a widely accepted and widely used tool especially in TLS, SSL, HTTPS etc.

A cryptographic hash (sometimes called 'digest') is a kind of 'signature' for a text or a data file. SHA-256 generates an almost-unique 256-bit (32-byte) signature for a text. In simple words if you give an input the terminal will give a 256-bit string. Let's take an example

SHA-256 hash calculator

SHA-256 produces a 256-bit (32-byte) hash value.

Data

SHA-256 hash

Hash added to your clipboard. Simply press ⌘+V, CTRL+V to paste.

So, if you give 'iamnoob' as an input you will get such an output. But before breaking it down we will talk about the key features of SHA 256.If we select a hash function it must be pretty special right? Damn! It should be and it is.

Without further ado we will look into the main features of SHA 256. But beware once you go SHA, you don't need to go far!!

Main features of SHA 256 in a classic list style are as follows.

Fixed Output Length:

SHA-256 generates a fixed-length output of 256 bits (32 bytes) regardless of the size of the input data. This fixed size makes it suitable for consistent use in cryptographic applications.

As we seen above iamnoob input gave an output as 5069b9fb1aa6f2ab07832269d29a1cbdae0fa2302daa5c5296 6fbe2ae4978f67

Any input will always give 256-bit long output

Deterministic Hashing:

For a given input, SHA-256 always produces the same hash. This consistency ensures reliability in verifying data integrity and authenticity. Which means no matter how many times you hash 'iamnoob' the output hash will always be the same.

Preimage Resistance: It is computationally infeasible to reverse-engineer the original input from its hash output. This property ensures the security of hashed data.

Let's say somebody found the above hash in your diary and wanted to know the input. Can they find your input? Answer is no, SHA 256 is a one-way hash function and cannot be reverse engineered. Technically it is reversible but the time required to do that is enormous, we are talking yearsss!!! And that is what makes SHA256 safe.

Collision Resistance:

SHA-256 is designed to minimize the possibility of two different inputs producing the same hash. This is crucial for applications like digital signatures and blockchain, where uniqueness is essential.

Avalanche Effect:

A small change in the input (even a single bit) results in a drastically different hash output. This sensitivity enhances the security of SHA-256 by making it unpredictable. Even if you change the input slightly the output hash will be totally different.

Iamnoob

SHA-256 hash calculator

SHA-256 produces a 256-bit (32-byte) hash value.

Data

iamanoob

SHA-256 hash

a7c9170281e66240cef50235ca9ce062c86adf0073fe54c41ca6e1b0ffbc36c2 5069b9fb1aa6f2ab07832269d29a1cbdae0fa2302daa5c5296 6fbe2ae4978f67

Iamanoob

a7c9170281e66240cef50235ca9ce062c86adf0073fe54c41ca6 e1b0ffbc36c2

Both hashes do not have the faintest of resemblance as our input was slightly modified.

High Computational Efficiency:

SHA-256 is optimized for performance and can process large amounts of data efficiently, making it suitable for high-speed applications.

Widely Adopted Standard:

As part of the SHA-2 family, SHA-256 is a widely accepted and well-tested standard for cryptographic hashing. It is used in protocols such as SSL/TLS, Bitcoin, and many secure systems.

Security Against Brute Force:

The 256-bit hash output offers a large key space, making brute-force attacks impractical. It would take an astronomical amount of computational effort to find a collision or pre-image.

Non-reversible:

SHA-256 hashes are one-way functions, meaning they cannot be decrypted back to the original input. This property is fundamental to its use in secure password storage and blockchain mining.

No Known Vulnerabilities: As of now, no practical vulnerabilities have been found in SHA-256, making it one of the most secure hash functions available for modern cryptographic needs.

These features collectively make SHA-256 a robust and reliable hash function that is critical to the security of numerous technologies, particularly in areas requiring data integrity, authentication, and non-repudiation.

Chapter-10

Block

We now have the necessary ingredients to create a block. As we said earlier, we have a digital ledger keeping track of transactions on the bitcoin network. These transactions do not come to blocks directly. The pending transaction comes and stays in a queue called 'Mempool'. From here on we call block creators as miners.

There are the two types of computers on the network, Miners and Nodes. Miners are the computers who create the blocks on the bitcoin blockchain and has a copy of the bitcoin blockchain. Nodes are computers which also keeps a copy of the bitcoin blockchain and verifies user transactions and places them in the mempool but does not create blocks. So, all miners are nodes but all nodes are not miners! Unfortunately, only miners get the reward. Nodes are on the bitcoin network just to enhance the safety of the network.

Consider Mempool as a bowl and whenever you need a transaction you can pick it up from the bowl. Each Bitcoin transaction requires a fee and this fee goes to the miner. So, a miner who creates a block will get fees of all transactions in that particular block and in the end the block reward. Bitcoin has a block size of 1MB, so a miner can add 1500-3000 transactions in a block depending on the Tx size.

Miner earnings =TX fees + Block reward.

Our digital ledger does not keep track of transactions in human language. This is where SHA 256 comes in. What a miner does is take transaction data from 'Mempool' and hashes it. Suppose there are 2000 Tx in a block then the miner will have 2000 hashes, right? But 2000 lines of hashes is cumbersome and not tidy. To shorten this bitcoin uses a system called 'Merkle tree'. Each individual hashes are considered as input and then hashed again and finally a single hash remains.

Check the image in the next page.

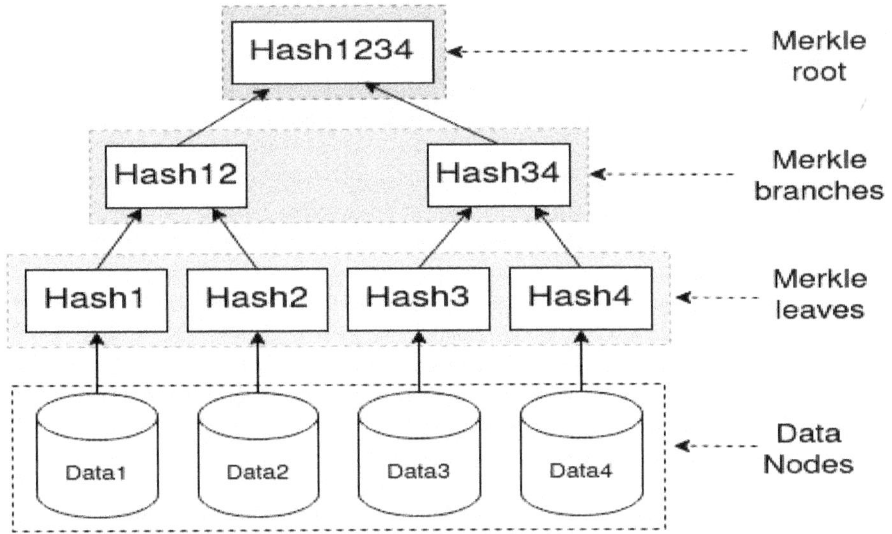

Here, in the above picture Data 1,2,3 & 4 are transactions from mempool. Hash 1,2,3 & 4 are the hashes of each transaction. In the above case Hash 1 & 2 are taken as input and hashed to obtain Hash 12. Similarly Hash 34 is obtained.

Again Hash 12 and 34 are taken as input to convert into Hash 1234 which is called the Merkle Root. So, of all the transactions in a block only a Merkle hash remains.

This also possesses a major advantage as well. A bad actor trying to reverse engineer the hash has now a single Merkle hash. He has to reverse engineer this particular hash to several individual transaction hashes. From these individual hashes he/she has to reverse engineer again to obtain the transaction data which takes enormous amounts of time.

The time taken to do this is what makes SHA 256 safe. Reverse engineering a hash in a thousand year is not worth it right? By the time it happens every party involved will be long gone.

A   block   has   few   other   data   as   well.

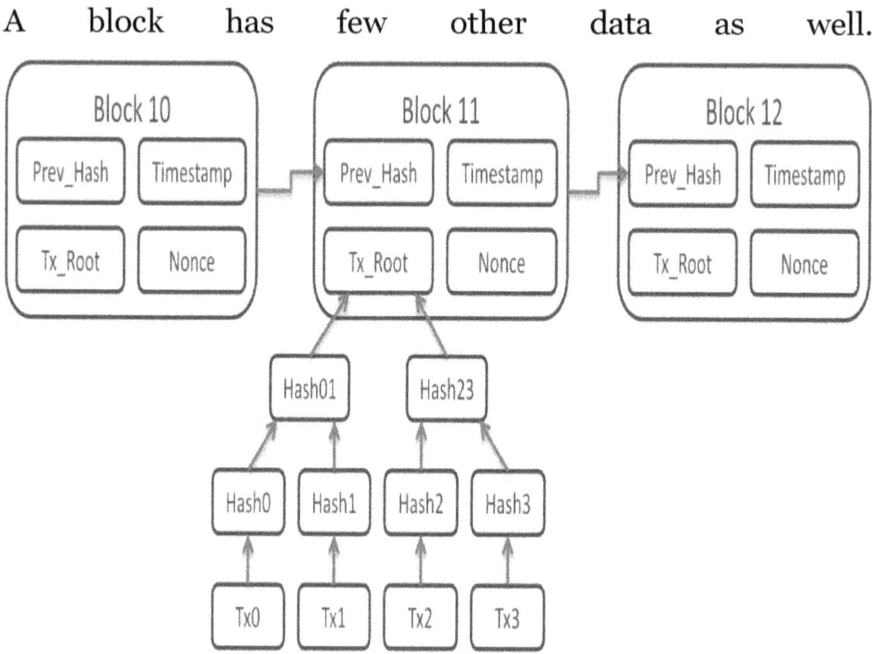

Concentrate on any one block. Say Block 10. This particular block has

-Previous hash

-Timestamp

-Tx root

-Nonce

- Previous hash is the final hash of the previous block when it was mined.

- Timestamp is the recorded time when the block was mined.
- Tx root as we spoke is the Merkle root of all the Tx in that block
- Nonce or number used once is the key for proof of work algorithm.

To mine a block, we need to solve the Byzantine Generals Problem—the challenge of ensuring that all nodes in a decentralized network reach consensus despite potential faults or malicious actors. This is where proof of work comes in.

Chapter-11

Proof of work

Proof work is an algorithm developed by Hal Finney in 2004 through the idea of 'Reusable proof of work' using 160-bit SHA-1. Bitcoin uses POW to obtain consensus. We talked about consensus in Chapter 8.

In a network like bitcoin every miner has a single goal of mining the block first and getting the block reward. Every miner will have his own version of excuses if somebody else claims the block. We built a decentralized system, so the title of the 'block creator' must be agreed unanimously.

Disagreement between miners arises from the fact that only one person can create a block and only one person will receive the reward. And everyone's competing to get the block reward. No person in this world who spends money for electricity will agree that someone else created the block right? We tackle this using Proof of Work (POW).

You all must be wondering that it's easy to take a few thousand transactions from the Mempool and hash it using SHA

256.Yes you are right!!That is the easiest part. You will definitely get the reward if you do the work but you have to solve a computational puzzle as well.

So now let us assume that you are a miner trying to solve the puzzle and you have selected as many transactions as you can and hashed it. You narrowed the hashes to one single Merkle Root as well. Now you are ready to solve the puzzle.

Main part of puzzle begins with 'Nonce' or number used once and 'Difficulty target'. Let us assume that Nonce starts with the value '0' and difficulty is '4'. What this means is that when you take all the data in a block and hash it you should get a final output hash starting with 4 zeroes.

We know that we cannot change any data in a block. Even a slight change can alter the output hash significantly. To achieve these 4 zeroes (difficulty target), we have the luxury to change the nonce to any number of our choice.

Let's say there is only one transaction in the block you were mining. You took this particular TX from Mempool and hashed it and you have an output hash '1234',

This example is solely for our case as we know that SHA 256 won't give an output 1234, it will always give a 256-bit output.

The nonce for the block is 'o' and the difficulty is '4'. So now you need an output hash with 4 zeros. We need previous block hash and time stamp as input as well. But for easier understanding we are using the Tx hash and nonce in the example.

You will start with an input

1234(hash of Tx)0(nonce)

Input-12340

Let us say you have the following output hash **5069b9fb1aa6f2ab07832269d29a1cbdae0fa2302daa5c52966fbe 2ae4978f67**

This doesn't qualify as it doesn't have 4 zeros in the beginning. The next step is to increment the nonce by 1.

Let's change the nonce to 1

1234(hash of Tx)1(Increment to nonce)

Input-12341

Output-

a7c9170281e66240cef50235ca9ce062c86adf0073fe54c41ca6e1b0 ffbc36c2

This also does not qualify as per the difficulty target.

Similarly, you will guess one after another until you obtain the required hash. So let us say you did *987654321* tries and you got the output

Input
1234(hash of Tx)987654321(nonce)

Output:0000b70281e66240cef50235ca9ce062c86adf0073fe54c4 1ca6e1b0ffbc36c2

Now you have 4 zeros and can create the block. But how will everyone agree unanimously?

For that, when the block is created you distribute the ledger data to the bitcoin blockchain. In this announcement instead of the Nonce value as 'o' you will have your ledger Tx hash which is the final Merkle root, timestamp, previous block hash and a nonce you guessed which was **987654321**.

Now anybody can use the nonce you gave and hash it to obtain 4 zeroes confirming your claim. Like that everyone reach consensus about the block creator and now you can add your wallet address and receive the block reward. This final Tx with all fess from the transactions in the block and block reward is called the **"Coinbase Transaction."**

Number of BTC received will be based on the last halving. So, for now it is 3.125 BTC.

So, the only advantage a miner can have is his computational power. The faster you can guess the faster you can mine the block. But what if a powerful machine joins the network?

 Let's say we can guess only once in a second and he can do 2 guesses in a second. So, no matter what we do he will find the proof of work in half the time. To prevent this disparity the difficulty is adjusted (increased or decreased) accordingly, usually after every 2016 blocks. The 10 min per block time means it will take 2 weeks. So, in two weeks' time the difficulty moves according to the computer power of the network or hash power. The new machine has two weeks of advantage and then he also has to find a way like us.

This secures the network as computer power increases network security increases and it makes it a level playing field for everyone.

Chapter- 12

Public and Private Keys

Now we are familiar with how bitcoin works. We exactly know how it comes to existence and what goes behind the mining process. All this is as good as nothing if we cannot store it safely and securely. That is why wallets plays a vital role in storing, maintaining and use of bitcoin and other cryptocurrencies.

To store bitcoin, we need a wallet app. There are a lot of wallets available today. Trust wallet, exodus wallet, Tangem wallet are all examples of wallets. But before we get into the various types of wallets we need to understand how wallets work.

Modern cryptocurrency wallets make the blockchain accessible to everyone. When cryptocurrency was first introduced, sending cryptocurrency was a mundane task that required entering long keys.

Today, the software does most of it for you. The first ever wallet belonged to the founder, Satoshi Nakamoto. The second wallet belonged to Hal Finney, who was in direct contact with Nakamoto and was the first to run the Bitcoin client software wallet. Satoshi sent him 10 bitcoins as a test, the first ever transaction on the bitcoin blockchain and the bitcoin craze began.

Now let us consider making a similar transaction on the network from a wallet to another wallet.

When you send a cryptocurrency:

First, you enter the recipient's wallet (address) and specify the amount to send. A wallet address like the image on the next page is a shorter version of the public key, typically represented as an alphanumeric string or QR code. It serves as the identifier for receiving funds and is unique to each wallet. Like a bank account number.

The wallet uses the private key to create a digital signature, proving that we own the funds and authorize the transaction. The transaction is picked up by the nodes and verifies it. Once validated, the transaction is then added to the block by miners, and the recipient's balance is updated.

As we said earlier, cryptocurrency wallets are the most essential tools for storing, sending, and receiving digital currencies like Bitcoin, Ethereum, and others. Unlike traditional wallets, which hold physical cash, crypto wallets do not store the actual cryptocurrency. Instead, they store cryptographic keys that grant access to your digital assets on the blockchain.

At the core of every cryptocurrency wallet are two cryptographic keys:

- **Public Key**
- **Private Key**

These two keys create and verify a;

- **Digital Signature**

A public key which can be shared is derived from the private key using a mathematical algorithm. It acts like our own bank account number, which can be shared publicly to receive cryptocurrency. The public key is then hashed to create the wallet address in such a way ensuring that even if the public key is exposed, the actual private key remains secure. One of the main features of the public key is that it allows anyone to verify a transaction without revealing the private key, ensuring transparency and security.

On the other hand, private key is a secret key that must be kept secure at any cost. It is used to generate digital signatures that authorize transactions. If someone gets access to your private key, they control all the funds associated with the corresponding public key. Private keys are typically represented as long alphanumeric strings or stored securely in the wallet using encryption.

A digital signature on the other hand is a cryptographic tool that ensures the integrity, authenticity, and non-repudiation of transactions in the cryptocurrency ecosystem. Here's how it works:

Signature Generation:

When a user initiates a transaction, a digital signature is created using the private key. The signature created is unique to that particular transaction and private key. Consider it as signing a physical cheque. But here the sign is unique for each Tx.

Verification:

The network verifies the digital signature by using the public key and digital signature together. When verifying the private key is not required.

If any part of the transaction data is altered after the signature is created, the signature becomes invalid. This ensures that the transaction cannot be tampered with.

So, a digital signature is like signing a cheque with a physical signature to prove it is you signing the transaction. Only difference here is that the digital signature unlike physical signatures is a set of 0 and 1 which changes every transaction and the public key is used to verify the signature is yours. I know it's confusing and might have gone above your head. But I am not gonna hang you up to dry. Let us break this down in a more English language way!!

In a cryptocurrency a wallet is created using Public Key Cryptography (PKC) also known as asymmetric cryptography. Unlike symmetric cryptography we have two keys here called a public key and a private key. Public key can be shared to anyone, the private key must be kept secret and safe as anybody with an access to the private key can decrypt any message created using the public key.

Asymmetric cryptography has its own benefits. For example, you met a girl and you want to send her an encrypted letter using symmetric encryption: that is an encryption with only one key. You write a wonderful romantic letter and encrypt it using the key and send her the letter. Upon receiving she asks you what the heck is this coded message. Now you let her know that "Babe it is an encrypted letter from my side and you can use my key when we meet to decrypt the message." She gets excited, you give her your key and she find the letter as a romantic gesture and now you guys are dating!

One fine day during your date she brings her sister as well to introduce you to her family one by one. Now you being a naughty player has eyes on her sister as well. Then you write another letter to her sister and impresses her with your Romance and deep knowledge and wisdom in Cryptography. Now you are having a wonderful life with the sisters.

One fine day, you receive an encrypted letter. You tried decrypting the message with your key and it worked. But the issue is you don't know which one sent you the letter. You decided enough is enough and you invite both of them for dinner. Your plan was to throw in a bit of the content of the letter in the middle of the dinner to find out who sent the letter.

Everything was going well as you planned but the other sister finds the letter in your device and she being the possessive lovely girlfriend decrypts the message with the key you gave her and finds out your double love life strategy. Now you are neck deep in and you're finished.

After this you decided to use asymmetric encryption where you hold the private key and you give public keys to the sisters. Now both of them can only read the messages but cannot send a message back. Each asymmetric key pair is unique, ensuring that a message encrypted using a private key can only be read by the person who possesses the corresponding public key.

If anyone of them wants to send a reply they have to create their own key pairs and encrypt using their private key and share their specific public key to you. So, now when you receive an anonymous letter you can try decrypting with one of two public keys from the sisters and now you know who sent the letter.

When it comes to cryptocurrency the private key is used to encrypt a transaction and create a digital signature. The signature along with message (Tx) is send to the network.

Private key +Tx data= signature

this signature is then verified by the public key. While verifying, the message + signature and public key is hashed to ensure that the message was signed by the owner itself. Take a look at the image .

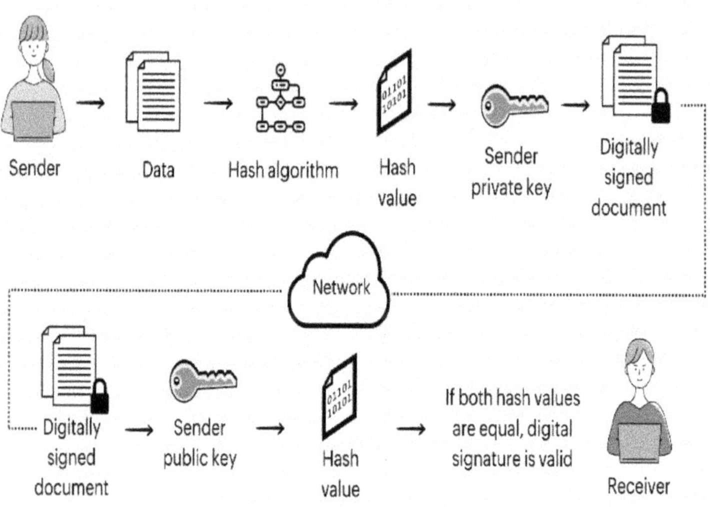

Thus, the use of key pairs gives a unique set of characteristics and capabilities that can be utilized to solve challenges inherent in other cryptographic techniques. This form of cryptography has become an important element of modern computer security, as well as a critical component of the growing cryptocurrency ecosystem.

Because asymmetric encryption algorithms generate key pairs that are mathematically linked, their key lengths are much longer than those used in symmetric cryptography. This longer length - typically between 1,024 and 2,048 bits - makes it extremely difficult to compute a private key from its public counterpart. One of the most common algorithms for asymmetric encryption in use today other than PKC is known as RSA.

In the RSA scheme, keys are generated using a modulus that is arrived at by multiplying two numbers (often two large prime numbers). In basic terms, the modulus generates two keys (one public that can be shared, and one private that should be kept in secret). The RSA algorithm was first described in 1977 by Rivest, Shamir, and Adleman (hence, RSA) and remains a major component of public key cryptography systems.

Another application of asymmetric cryptography algorithms is that of authenticating data through the use of digital signatures. Basically speaking, a digital signature is a hash created using the data in a message. When that message is sent, the signature can be checked by the recipient using the sender's public key. This way, they can authenticate the source of the message and ensure that it has not been tampered with. In some cases, digital signatures and encryption are applied together, meaning the hash itself may be encrypted as part of the message. It should be noted, however, that not all digital signature schemes use encryption techniques, Bitcoin does not use encryption to create public and private keys. Satoshi opted for an algorithm called Elliptical Curve Digital Signature Algorithm (ECDSA).

Chapter 13

Elliptical curve digital signature Algorithm (ECDSA)

Cryptocurrency is a technology where security is vital and Satoshi chose **ECDSA (Elliptic Curve Digital Signature Algorithm)** to generate digital signatures.

ECDSA is used to create digital signatures on many blockchains, including Bitcoin and Ethereum. The end goal is same: only the wallet owner who holds the private key shall have the power and right to sent a Tx and not anyone else.

In this section we will explore ECDSA in detail. We will try to break down its working, advantages and disadvantages.

So what is ECDSA?

ECDSA stands for **Elliptic Curve Digital Signature Algorithm**. ECDSA is a type of **public-key cryptography** that uses elliptic curves to generate digital signature. ECDSA allows the creation of a unique digital signature solely used to prove the authenticity of a message or transaction.

As we know Public-key cryptography is based on a pair of keys: a **public key** and a **private key**. The public key is used to encrypt or verify data, while the private key is used to decrypt or sign data. ECDSA specifically provides a method for **signing** data, creating a unique signature that is linked to the transaction and the private key of the signer.

Let us see how it works.

ECDSA is based on **elliptic curve cryptography (ECC)**, which is a type of public-key cryptography that uses the algebraic structure of elliptic curves over finite fields. Here's a simplified breakdown of how ECDSA works:

So, what the heck is elliptic curves?

Elliptic curves have (almost) nothing to do with ellipses, so first put ellipses and conic sections out of your thoughts. Elliptic curves appear in many diverse areas of mathematics, ranging from number theory to complex analysis, and from cryptography to mathematical physics.

An Elliptic Curve is a curve given by an equation of the form

$$Y^2 = X^3 + Ax + b$$

Let's take an example, all math geeks hold your horses. This explanation is for people like me and others!

$Y^2=x^3-1$

We need to assign values to x and obtain values for y and plot it on a graph. For people who need further explanation check next page.

$$y^2 = x^3 - 1$$
$$y = \pm\sqrt{x^3-1}$$

for $x = 1$
$$y^2 = 1^3 - 1 = 0$$
$$y = 0$$
$$(x, y) = (1, 0)$$

for $x = 2$
$$y^2 = 2^3 - 1 = 8 - 1 = 7$$
$$y = \pm\sqrt{7} = 2.645$$
$$(x, y) = (2, 2.645)$$

for $x = 3$
$$y^2 = 3^3 - 1 = 27 - 1$$
$$y = \pm\sqrt{26} = 5.099$$
$$(x, y) = (3, 5.099)$$

Example graphs of such elliptic curve equations are on the next page.

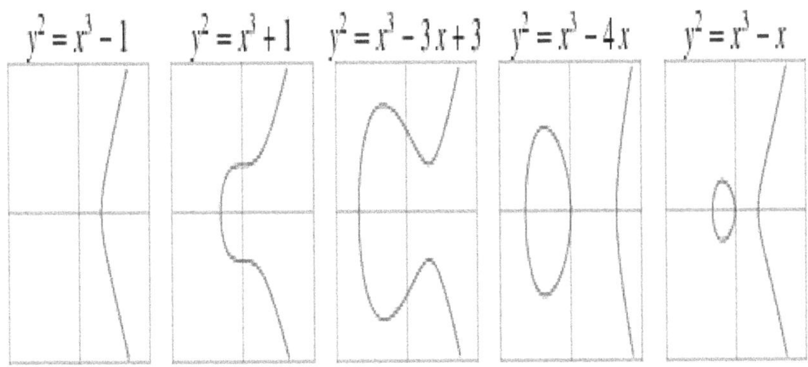

Bitcoin uses an elliptic curve called **secp256k1** which has an equation **Y²=X³+7 (This also is in the form Y²=X³+Ax+b, here a=0, b=7)** and it looks like this.

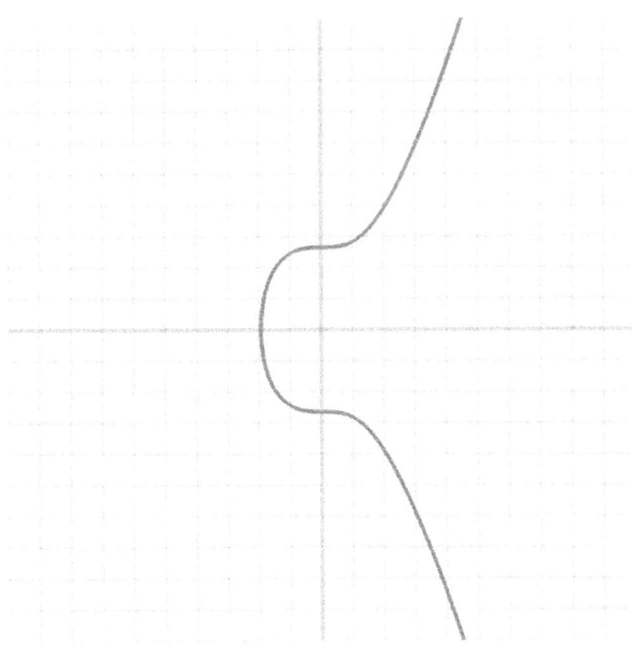

Elliptical curve points have some specialty. Like adding numbers, we can add points on the elliptic curve.

Let us take a point P and Q on the curve.

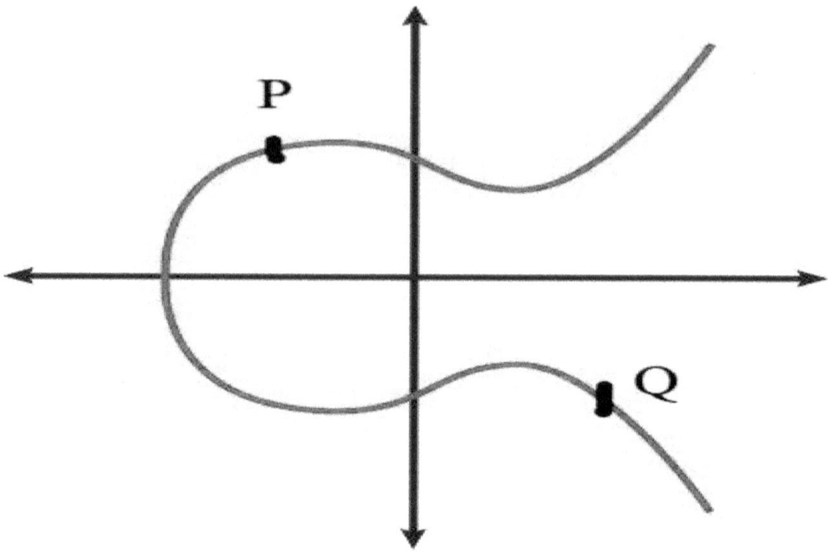

Join both the points P & Q. The line should cut a point on the curve. Draw a line from this curve through the X axis. This point is called R.

By addition means **P+Q=R**

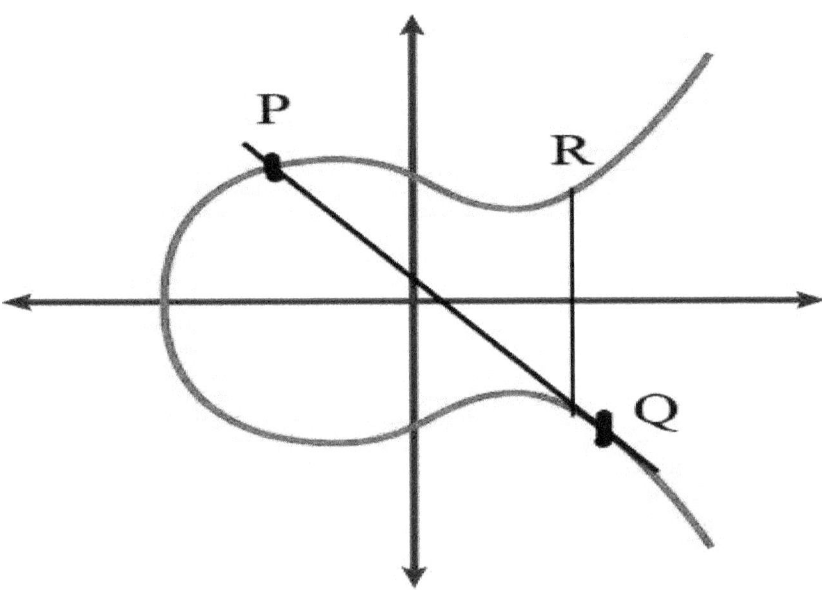

But to do efficient cryptography rather than adding two arbitrary points we add the same point by drawing a tangent to a point on the curve. This is how multiplication is done with elliptic curves, by adding a point to itself 'n' number of times.

Let us consider the same point P and draw a tangent. The tangent will intersect the curve. Draw a perpendicular at that point through the X axis. This perpendicular will meet the curve and this point is called P+P that is 2P.

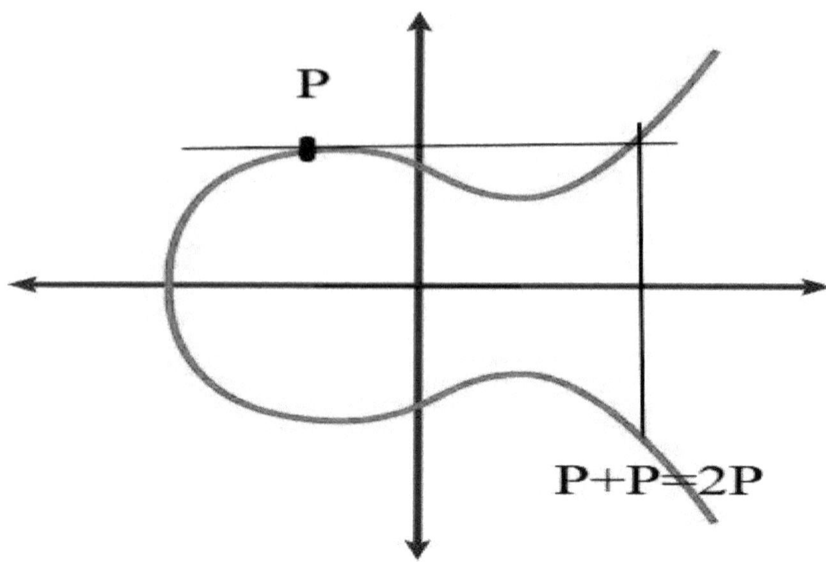

We can continue to add P to itself to calculate 4P,5P etc. by drawing tangents from 2P, 3P and so on. So, this means that 10P should take 9 additions right.

10P=P+P+P+P+P+P+P+P+P+P but we can do this in 4 steps.

This is possible through a formula

nP+rP=(n+r) P

4P+6P= (4+6) P=10P

So, the easiest way to calculate 10P is

P+P=2P

2P+2P=4P

4P+4P=8P

8P+2P=10P

But how many operations will it take to calculate xP if x is a 256-bit integer. In this case x can be a very large integer

X e(0<z<1.1579209e+77) But it turns out it will take only 510 operations. Let me explain.

The binary expansion of x will have 256 elements. So that is up to 2^{255}. So, the addition will be

x+x+x+x+x..............250 more x

That means to compute **xP it will take 255+255=510 steps.**

Keep xP in mind we will need it very soon.

Math geeks wake up!!!It is time.

Key Generation:

First, a pair of keys is generated: a **private key** and a **public key**. The private key as we said earlier is a random number, while the public key is derived from the private key using elliptic curve mathematics. This process ensures that the public key can be publicly shared, but the private key remains secret and is used for signing.

To calculate private key, we use a random number generator. Bitcoin has its own random number generator built in. This random number will be a point on the elliptic curve similar to 'P' from our example. This private key is represented as a 256-bit number.

Public key is derived from $K=k* G$

where **K** is the public key, **k** is the private key and **G** is a generator point. **G** will be number which is fixed. Similar to our example we multiply **k G** number of times by drawing tangents. **K** or the public key will be a point on the elliptic curve. Its **(x, y)** co-ordinates are taken as the value of the public key.

Here's an example of a 256-bit ECDSA public key (on the secp256k1 curve): (x, y) co-ordinates.

0x5cbdf8a0bfa4b4a74175d28f7f63a1fe5e1b5482ab1b91cf b7a47260d5578c25

0x6a8d2676b8a84c9a47ecce27f1da6c5c08152b0c32b3e2 efcfa0c75a73b1c27b

The public key will be the combination of both.

0x5cbdf8a0bfa4b4a74175d28f7f63a1fe5e1b5482ab1b91cf b7a47260d5578c250x6a8d2676b8a84c9a47ecce27f1da6c 5c08152b0c32b3e2efcfa0c75a73b1c27b

If we know 2 out of 3 variables, we can find the missing one right. But fortunately, although the relation between **K** and **k** is fixed it can only be calculated in one direction and is called the **"Trapdoor Function"** in ECDSA. Thus, sharing a public key will not expose the private key.

To create the bitcoin address, the public key is hashed using **SHA256** and then the SHA 256 output is hashed again using **RIPEMD160** or **RACE Integrity Primitives Evaluation Message Digest**, producing a 160-bit output.

Address= RIPEMD160 (SHA256 (K)).

Signing a Transaction (Creating a Signature):

Creating a digital signature using elliptic curve is a two-step process. First, we create a value called r, and then a value called s. To obtain r, a random number 'k' is generated. We do multiplication on the curve and obtain a point on the curve.

-r is derived from the x-coordinate of this point on the elliptic curve.

-s is computed using a formula that involves the private key, the message hash, and r

s= (r * public key+ hash of Tx data) / r

Verifying the Signature:

A Node has to verify the signature. These nodes understand that a signature is created using a private key and the only thing they ensures is that the public key shared corresponds to the private key which signed the Tx. Verification of such a signature is also a two-step process

The verification process involves:

1. First, r is plotted on the curve and the node multiplies **r*Tx** hash, this will give the node a big number. This number is added onto the elliptic curve. Multiplication done and they obtain a point on the elliptic curve.
2. Then the node multiplies **r*s** and computes again on the curve. The magic of elliptic curves is if the signature is valid all three points coincide on the same line.

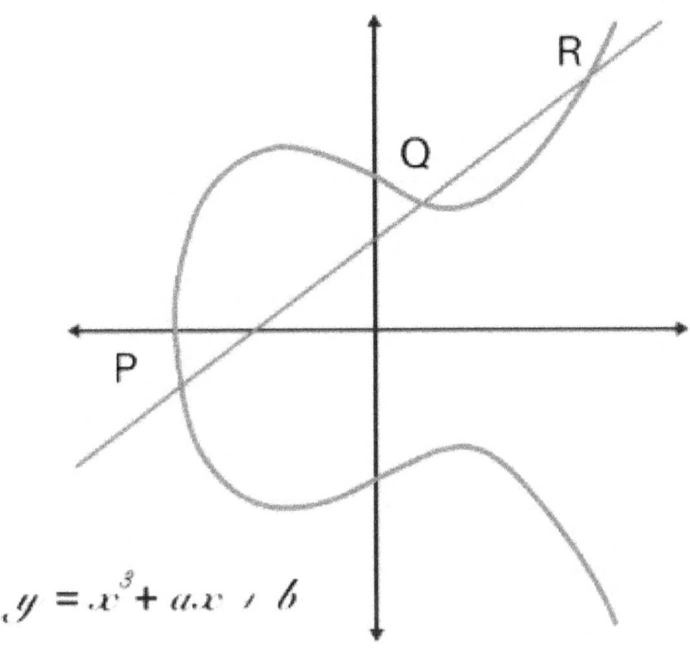

Why is ECDSA Used in Cryptocurrencies?

The primary reason ECDSA is used in cryptocurrencies like Bitcoin is its security. Elliptic curve cryptography, is one of the most secure algorithms for generating public-private key pairs. Moreover, ECDSA is more efficient than other signature algorithms, such as RSA, for the same level of security. Meaning that ECDSA provides a higher level of security with smaller key sizes.

For example, a 256-bit key in ECDSA offers security equivalent to a 3072-bit key in RSA. That is the difference in key sizes and it makes ECDSA more efficient in terms of storage and processing power, which is important for blockchain networks that handle a large number of transactions.

The shorter key lengths to achieve the same level of security is thus very important.

As any system ECDSA also comes with a set of drawbacks. They are as follows.

1. ECDSA generates a unique random number (k) for each signature. If the random number is not truly random or is reused, it can have catastrophic affects and can lead to security vulnerabilities. Close your eyes for this!! In the worst-case scenario, reusing the same random number across different transactions can allow an attacker to calculate the private key, compromising the entire wallet. That is like giving someone access to your bank account. But You can chill!! This is a 0.000000001% possibility

2. Although ECDSA signatures are smaller than RSA signatures, they still require two values (r and s) for each signature. This means the total signature size is larger than the hash size (32 bytes for Bitcoin). This is a concern as in certain environments with strict data size limits.

3.While ECDSA is currently considered secure, it is not resistant to **quantum computing**. Once large-scale quantum computers become available, they could potentially break the elliptic curve cryptography used in ECDSA, rendering it insecure. You will hear this quantum computer crap every now and then in crypto. But we have devs on our side. We have already developed quantum resistive ledgers. Let the nerds take over this issue, we sit back and watch the show as it unfolds.

We must talk about the alternatives as well.

While ECDSA is widely used in Bitcoin and many other blockchains, there are potential alternatives:

1.   EdDSA   (Edwards-curve   Digital   Signature Algorithm):
EdDSA is a new kid on the block. It has a robust signature scheme that also uses elliptic curve cryptography but has some advantages over ECDSA, which include faster verification and resistance to certain vulnerabilities like weak random number generation.

2. RSA: RSA is one of the most widely used digital signature algorithms after ECDSA. But but but! To ensure the same level of safety RSA demands a larger key size which will eat up space in a block.

3. Schnorr Signatures: Schnorr signatures are another alternative that offers higher efficiency and security compared to ECDSA. Bitcoin developers have been in love with Schnorr signatures for quiet sometime now and it is already added to Bitcoin via Taproot upgrade.

Now we know why ECDSA is considered as an important cryptographic algorithm to ensure the security and authenticity of transactions in blockchain networks. Its efficiency, strong security, and widespread adoption have made it the preferred choice for securing digital assets in many cryptocurrencies, including Bitcoin. However, like all cryptographic algorithms, it has limitations, such as its vulnerability to weak random number generation and its lack of quantum resistance.

Understanding how ECDSA works and why it's used in cryptocurrency is crucial for anyone involved in Bitcoin. It is one of the main components which keeps our Bitcoin safe; both in our wallet and when transacting.

Chapter-14

Wallets

Now you all must have an idea of how wallets work. The role of wallets in storing and managing any crypto asset is undeniable. Unlike traditional banking systems, in a cryptocurrency like Bitcoin the user is responsible for storing their respective private keys safe and securely. To achieve the same, we need secure digital wallets. These wallets are apps or software which allow us users to send, receive, store and manage our crypto on the blockchain. We must choose a wallet that meets our requirements and it must be safe and secure too. However, it is easier said than done. Choosing a right wallet can be challenging today as we have a wide array of wallets available, each with its own set of features, convenience and drawbacks in terms of safety and control.

So, it is quintessential that we talk about the various types of wallets available in the modern-day crypto space. I hope I will make your wallet selection decision easier and effortless. So, without further ado let us begin!!

In a broader context wallet can be divided into three major categories. They are: irrespective of the order hardware, software and paper wallets. However, they can be further divided into cold and hot wallets based on how they work.

Software wallets are the most accessible, most convenient and free to use, whereas hardware wallets are the most secure. Paper wallets as the name suggest is printed on a piece of paper and are now obsolete.

As we mentioned earlier, we don't store crypto in our wallets. They are like your keys to your house. Your whole stuff is inside the house and you need the key to get access. Here the key is your wallet which has the cryptographic keys (private and public key pair) and the house is the respective blockchain.

Wallets can be classified as cold or hot wallets based on the method in which they store your private key.

Hot vs Cold wallets

The main difference between them is whether they are connected to the internet or not.

Hot Wallets

These types of wallets are always connected to the internet. Thus, it allows quick access and ease the transaction process. These wallets are ideal for people who needs frequent access to their crypto or users who actively trade crypto.

Types of hot wallets

Software wallets (a.k.a desktop wallets)

A desktop or a software wallet is a software which can be installed on a computer to manage crypto assets. It gives you full access to your keys and is secure to use also. The major caveat is that the private key is stored on the device which is the computer in which the software is installed. This pose a major flow as it will expose your private key if the device is compromised.

Examples of software wallets are Exodus, Electrum, Bitcoin Core etc.

Mobile wallets

Mobile wallets as the name suggests is an app which can be installed in a smartphone. This type of wallets is similar to desktop wallets but now you have more convenience as phones are a part of the human body nowadays. They possess the same risk as desktop wallets.

Examples of mobile wallets are moonlet, Trust wallet, Coinomi etc. Some wallets like Exodus have both desktop and mobile versions.

Web Wallets

In this type of wallets, the private keys are stored on remote servers. One can access this wallet on any device with an internet connection using their user id and password. These are way riskier than mobile wallets as we don't hold the keys to our crypto. The number 1 saying in crypto is "Not your keys, not your crypto."

Examples of web wallets are Blockchain.com and Coinbase wallet.

Exchange wallets

As the name suggests these wallets are maintained by exchanges and they hold the private keys for crypto stored in their respective exchange. These types of wallets are chosen generally by traders who actively trade crypto on a day-to-day basis. But always remember "Not your keys, not your crypto." If the exchange gets hacked or they go bust or bankrupt or whatever you wanna call it, you can kiss your crypto goodbye as well.

Recent collapse of FTX is an example. Also, recent hack in an Indian exchange named wazirx might be an eye opener for you. Examples of exchange wallets are Binance, Kraken, Kucoin etc.

Cold wallets

As the name suggests these are cold af! and are not connected to the internet. This type of wallets is ideal for people who are planning to hold their crypto for a long period of time and does not plan to touch them in the foreseeable future.

Types of cold wallets

Hardware wallets

Hardware wallets are physical devises designed specifically for one purpose and one purpose only storing private keys. They store your private key in a secure element chip inside the device which self-destructs if tampered with. These secure element chips come with their own standard such as ELA 5 or ELA 6 etc.

Examples of hardware wallets are Ledger, Tangem, Trezor etc.

Unlike Hot wallets these are not free to use. Hardware starts from 50$ and goes till 500$. I recommend investing in a hardware wallet if you are going to stay in crypto for long. I assume that you wouldn't be buying or reading this book if you weren't planning to stay in this wonderland.

Some hardware wallets need internet connection though. Whenever you send a transaction you have to physically sign the transaction using buttons or via NFC in the hardware wallet. And these wallets will be protected by a password as well. So, basically the device must be in the sender's hand to execute the Tx. This feature is what makes hardware wallets more secure.

In a software wallet if you click send there are no additional steps involved. The software or the particular app will fetch your private key from the device and sign the Tx for you on your behalf.

But what if you need a wallet which has no connection to the internet; enter Air gapped wallets

Air-Gapped wallets

These wallets are similar to hardware wallets but instead of relying on an internet connection these wallets use QR codes to send and receive crypto. It comes with all the above-mentioned features of the hardware wallets.

And for your information, in modern day software wallets like Trust wallet and Exodus we can create additional wallets by connecting our hardware wallets to it. This is done generally if a token or crypto you purchased is not supported by your hardware wallet but can be stored on the software counterpart instead.

Based on the above classification we have new set of wallet categories as well. They are:

Custodial Wallets

These wallets can be either hot or cold wallets but the private keys are managed by a custodian. They are generally user friendly and easy to use and most of them has recovery option too if we lose our password. Although it seems convenient but you already know the risks associated with this right? "Not your keys, not your crypto."

Some custodian wallet services provide insurance for your crypto as well. So, if you don't want to take the headache of storing crypto you can go that route.

Non-Custodial Wallets

Non-Custodial as the name suggests is the wallets in which we store our private keys and have full access to the wallets. These wallets may be either hot or cold wallets.

Having a non-custodial wallet is like operating our own bank. "With great power comes great responsibility." We are responsible for our private keys. If we lose it, we cannot go to the cops or court for retrieval. Once it is lost it is lost forever.

The idea of this chapter is not to scare you away. But to assist you in choosing a wallet. Choosing a right wallet is essential and the first step to secure our crypto. The wallet you select must be secure as we are putting our hard-earned inflated bastard on the line for financial freedom. There is surely a learning curve to it but you will get their eventually. Watch one or two tutorials on YouTube about hardware wallets and you will be up and running in no time.

Budget is also a factor when considering the type of wallets but I ensure you the money you are gonna spend is totally worth it. I have been using hardware wallets for the past five years and I had no issues with them. For beginners I recommend a wallet called Tangem as it is easy to setup and use. Find that tutorial and enjoy your time in crypto.

If hot wallets are convenient then cold wallets are secure so decide for yourself. Our primary goal is to safeguard our private keys with our dear life. Now we move to the next important thing about wallets "Seed Phrases".

Chapter-15

Seed Phrase

What will you do if you wallet device go bust? and you didn't backup your keys as well.

It is cumbersome and difficult to store large private keys securely as a backup. Don't worry now we have a feature called **seed phrase.** Whether you are a Bitcoin maximalist or an Ethereum lover you must know what a seed phrase is.

In this chapter we will look closely into seed phrase, its history, use case and their management. Whether you are a beginner or seasoned investor seed phrase is the one concept you cannot overlook.

So, what the heck is a seed phrase?

A seed phrase also known as **recovery phrase** or a **mnemonic seed** is set of 12, 18 or 24 words in a sequence which acts as a backup of the private key. Most of the modern wallets use seed phrases and if you lose the phrase, you lose access to your crypto if your device is damaged or lost.

In other words, a seed phrase is a human readable representation of the private keys associated with your respective wallets. And it acts as the one and only backup for your wallet, if your wallet is lost, stollen or damaged.

A seed phrase is created when we first set up a wallet. It is our responsibility to ensure that the sequence is backed up. Most of the wallets while setting up will ask to type the phrase again so that is a plus for noobs. When we migrate to a new device or wallet, the seed phrase must be entered in the exact sequence as it was first generated.

The words chosen are part of a Bitcoin Improvement Protocol called BIP39 which is a dictionary of 2048 words. The words are so selected so that no words share resemblance to any other in the list and no word will have the same four alphabets. Also, every word can be easily guessed by your tiny brain after reading the first four alphabets if it has more than four alphabets of course!!!

So "whomever who possess the seed phrase is worthy of accessing the wallet" and the crypto gods are brutal, if you tell your so thought soulmate the seed phrase, he/she has now full access. Crypto churns your brain and you will surely have second thoughts about whom you trust the most haha!!!

Jokes apart we know seed phrase comes out from the BIP39 standard. Unfortunately, the words are created for us, we don't have the power to choose our own seed. This is to prevent collision of same seed in two different wallets.

The private key for your wallet is created from the seed phrase. This is achieved by assigning each word a binary code and all the words can be hashed together to create a private public key pair.

We already talked about the types of wallets as per storage of private keys. That was for laymen. We are crypto pioneers and we classify wallets on the basis of how the private key is generated. So, strap your seatbelts, it is time for a ride!!

As we said the seed phrase is used to generate the private key (or keys) for your wallet. Wallet software follows a process called **Hierarchical Deterministic (HD) Wallets** to create a tree-like structure of private and public keys, all derived from the seed phrase. This means that your seed phrase can generate all of your private keys, and in turn, all of the public addresses you use to send or receive funds.

We talked about creating a public and private key pair using ECDSA, that type of wallet is called a **non-deterministic wallet**. A deterministic wallet is a wallet with a seed phrase. The seed phrase is sequential set words which act as a translation for a 256-bit code called the 'Root Key.' That 256-bit code creates the public and private key pair.

Using a seed phrase we can create multiple accounts. This is possible using a derivation path. The 256-bit code is the same for every account because the seed phrase remains the same.

Let us take M/44"/60/4/0 as a derivation path and

5eb00bbddcf069084889a8ab9155568165f5c681f284a8d846 d21db2fdcb3a4e3ba4ba5b8677d649dedb3ce2b2766dd4fdc5f 03d15e8a1e7d93ccf8c6207bf07 is the root key for a 12-word seed mentioned below.

spirit supply whale amount human item harsh scare congress discovers talent hamster.

Note: **When recovering a wallet, the seed phrase must be entered in the same sequence**.

The above derivation path is for one account (one public and private key pair). For the next account only the derivation path changes may be M/44"/60/4/1

For the next one M/44"/60/4/2 so on and so forth.

Long story short when you create a new wallet, the wallet software will generate the seed phrase. This seed phrase is then used to generate your private keys in a specific order, which corresponds to public wallet addresses. The seed phrase doesn't need to store all the private keys; rather, it's a representation of them. This allows you to derive any number of addresses from the same seed phrase.Let us take it to the next level!!!Here is how it sounds in technical terms.

First you generate a 128bit-256bit entropy also called random data using a cryptographically secure random number generator. The same entropy we created is turned into either 12, 18 or 24 words using the reliable BIP39 standard word list.

The seed phrase is then hashed using an algorithm called PBKDF2, which is a key derivation function which gives a derivation path like the above example we took. We already know that the derivation path can create several private keys.

Hence, we can create 'n' number of public key private key pairs from a single seed phrase. As we said earlier the 2048 words are so selected so that no words are similar to each other such as "woman" or 'women'. words start with same four alphabets.

The security of the seed phrase is based on the probability itself. 12-word sequence from a 2048-word catalogue!! That is $\mathbf{2048^{12}}$ possibilities that corresponds to $\mathbf{5.44x10^{39}}$ possibilities· Now think about a 24-word seed phrase.

So, from an investor stand point seed phrase is like the password to our bank accounts. But unlike traditional systems we don't have a forgot password toggle. We are decentralized and if something goes south, we might as well head for south and self-destruct!

But if you successfully store the seed phrase you can restore the wallet anytime and anyplace as per your wish. On the positive side that is what crypto offers, 100% ownership. For the first time in the history of mankind we have an asset that we own fully. An asset which cannot be touched by anybody if we took proper precaution.

As the bitcoin whisperer it is my duty to suggest ways to store seed phrases safely with a bonus tip from my own experience. Here we go;

Write It Down on Paper:

While it might seem like an inconvenience, writing your seed phrase on paper is one of the most secure methods of backup. Paper doesn't rely on electricity, is immune to hacking attempts, and is portable. Make sure you store the paper in a safe place—preferably in a fireproof and waterproof container, such as a safe.

Avoid Digital Copies:

Storing your seed phrase digitally, whether in a text file, email, or cloud storage, increases the risk of it being compromised through hacking or theft. It's highly recommended to avoid storing your seed phrase on your computer or online.

Backup and Redundancy:

Store multiple copies of your seed phrase in different secure locations. Consider using a metal backup of your seed phrase, which is more durable than paper and less prone to damage from fire or water. Never rely on a single backup method.

Avoid Sharing Your Seed Phrase:

Your seed phrase is the key to your wallet. Never share it with anyone, and be cautious about phishing attempts where scammers may attempt to trick you into revealing your seed phrase. Always ensure you are interacting with the official software or hardware wallet provider.

Use Multi-Signature Wallets for Added Security: multi-signature wallets require multiple private keys (from multiple devices or users) to authorize a transaction. This can be a good way to secure your funds in case your seed phrase is compromised. For example, you could store your seed phrase on multiple devices or in multiple secure locations, and require two or more signatures to spend

One thing I do is I change the sequence of words. Let me explain!!!!

1.carpet

2.cat

3.*flower*

4.*chair*

5.*foot*

6.*river*

7.*make*

8.*image*

9.*amazing*

10.*three*

11.*say*

12.*shoe*

This is a 12-word phrase. Suppose let us say your lucky number is 3. What I do is I write the third word as the 12th word.

1.*carpet*

2.*cat*

3.*chair*

4.*foot*

5.river

6.make

7.image

8.amazing

9.three

10.say

11.shoe

12.Flower

You can do this with multiple numbers as well. So even if somebody finds your phrase, they cannot get access to your wallet. This way you can store it digitally as well.

However, the responsibility of safeguarding your seed phrase ultimately lies with you, and failure to do so could result in the permanent loss of your cryptocurrency. So, its high time that you guys bring maturity to the table haha!!

Jokes aside, as you venture further into the world of digital currencies, remember that security is an ongoing process, and your seed phrase is the foundation of that security and you will eventually reach there and will be a crypto pro.

Chapter-16

Unspent Transaction output (UTXO)

In our traditional banking system whenever a transaction is done, the money is subtracted from the sender and added to the beneficiary. Nothing actually moves through the network; it is just basic addition and subtraction. This type of balance keeping is called an **account-based model**.

In Bitcoin however we approach things differently. We have a model to keep track of balances called **UTXO or unspent transaction output**. UTXO plays a vital role in Tx validation, tracking balances and also prevents double spending. We mentioned under DLT that Bitcoin uses other methods to prevent double spending. UTXO is the main security guard who prevents double spending on the Bitcoin blockchain.

In this chapter we will try to breakdown the UTXO model in Bitcoin, compare it with the traditional account-based model. Understanding UTXO is like learning how banks keep their books secure. Get your popcorn, sit back and enjoy!!!

The term Unspent Transaction Output or UTXO is the Bitcoin balance in a transaction which can be used for future transactions.

We already mentioned that bitcoin transactions are not account based. In Bitcoin transactions, we have inputs and outputs. Once a transaction is verified the outputs become the UTXO. Let us take an example.

- Alice receives 0.5 BTC from Bob, creating a UTXO of 0.5 BTC.
- Alice later wants to send 0.3 BTC to Charlie. Alice will use her 0.5 BTC UTXO as an input, and create two outputs:
- 0.3BTC to Charlie. &
- 0.2 BTC (change) to herself.

In this example, Alice's transaction is spending her 0.5 BTC UTXO and creating new UTXOs for Charlie and herself.

So instead of addition and subtraction we take the UTXO required for the Tx. Here Alice has a balance of 0.5 BTC and she needs to transfer 0.3 BTC to Charlie. The network takes the balance (UTXO) sends 0.3 to Charlie and sends back the remaining 0.2 to Alice. Once the transactions are verified the outputs become UTXO. So, now Alice has an UTXO of 0.2 BTC.

So, whenever a user wants to carry out a transaction they give their UTXO as input in a new transaction and after the verification receives the unspent Bitcoin back to the wallet.

Let us put into technical words for Satoshi's sake!

A Bitcoin transaction typically comprises of

- **Inputs**-These are the references to the previous UTXOs from prior transactions.
- **Outputs**-The outputs after verification becomes UTXO for both sender and receiver.

That means while executing a transaction the input will have multiple UTXO from previous transactions. The input shall be such that it must be equal to or less than the input UTXOs. Remaining Bitcoins will be sent back to the sender as a new UTXO after verification.

We can call our wallet balance as a UTXO set if we have sent or receive Bitcoin more than one time. Let us comeback to the double spending issue. Every time a transaction is executed on the Bitcoin blockchain, it is the duty of nodes to validate the transaction. Validity of a transaction is based on the following factors;

- The input references are valid and unspent UTXOs

- The transaction does not exceed the value of the input UTXOs
- Digital signature is verified

Likewise, a transaction will only be validated if it meets all of the above-mentioned protocol rules. A violation in any one will result in rejection. Through this we mitigate the need of a central authority to track balances and we stay decentralized and secure.

So, whenever you hear someone say that we don't store crypto in our wallets you can elaborate on that. "Yes, babe we only store the private keys and the UTXO list from past transactions." Whenever we receive Bitcoin, the wallet adds the new UTXO to your list and whenever we send Bitcoin the wallet selects one or more UTXOs as inputs for the transaction. Bitcoin's proof of work consensus also ensures that the UTXO set is accurate and up-to-date across all nodes in the network.

This process where the wallet selects the appropriate UTXOs is called **"coin selection"** This is to ensure that appropriate UTXOs are picked to avoid **"fragmentations"** in your wallet.

When you receive multiple small transactions over the course of time there will be several tiny UTXOs, this is referred to as **fragmentation.** We cannot do anything about receiving but we sure can prevent UTXO fragmentation by selecting the required UTXO while sending Bitcoin.

One of the key benefits of the UTXO model is that it increases user privacy. Since it is UTXO based it is difficult for an observer to know the exact amount of Bitcoin a user holds just by looking at the address.

Having said that however, the bitcoin blockchain is transparent. That means an observer can view the transaction history associated with that wallet address. To prevent this wallet now change your Bitcoin address once you receive a transaction. And don't worry the old address will not be deleted it will still work. Seems like it is not your day-to-day bank account number right. Haha! Life and Bitcoin can be full of surprises.

However, one major drawback of UTXO model when compared with the traditional account-based model is fungibility. Fungibility is the property of an asset where each unit is interchangeable with another unit of same value. In an account-based model fungibility is straight forward right. However, in the UTXO model some UTXO might be tainted. If a UTXO was used in any illicit activity that might cause it to taint. You can definitely spend the UTXO but it can be tracked through the block explorer.

While the UTXO model can be complex and tough to wrap around but it enables our currency to stay secure and decentralized, and guess what since inception we never had a double spent on our blockchain. Every bit of tech in Bitcoin is there and there for a reason. A well thought and well-prepared dish. And I hope I was successful in breaking down UTXO to you folks.

We have one more concept to breakdown called "Bitcoin Script".

Chapter- 17

Bitcoin Script: The language of Bitcoin Transactions.

Bitcoin Script is stack-based programming language designed to validate Bitcoin transactions efficiently and securely. Unlike general purpose programming languages like Java or Python, Bitcoin script is not turing complete. This was done deliberately to prevent the risk of infinite loops and other potential vulnerabilities that could compromise the Bitcoin network.

We talked about private and public keys and digital signature, and its necessity to carry out a transaction. Bitcoin Script brings in a few more elements, to be specific two elements to ensure the transaction is valid or not. They are locking script (ScriptPubkey) and unlocking script (Scriptsig).

Let me explain!!

What this means is that when we carry out a transaction, we lock the bitcoin we send. For the receiver to unlock it and spend again he needs his private key associated with the public key to which the bitcoin was send.

To execute this, we have codes called **"Operators" or "OP_ codes".** We will be talking about five scripts in this chapter.

- **Pay to PubKey**
- **Pay to PubKey Hash**
- **Pay to Multisig**
- **Pay to Script Hash**
- **Return**

We need code examples to survive this chapter so sit tight.

So, there are two important elements ScriptPubkey and scriptSig.

scriptPubkey is used to lock the bitcoin while sending and scriptSig used to unlock the bitcoin to spent it. However, a locking script may not always have a PubKey in it and an unlocking script may not Sig (signature) in it, so they are often referred to as Locking and Unlocking script.

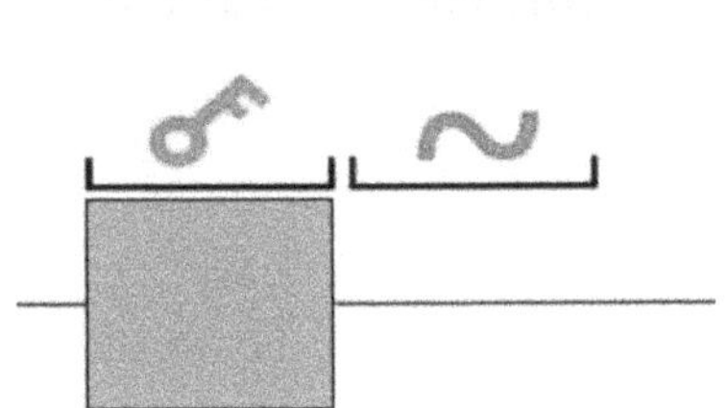

Here the sender's public key is the locking script and the signature is called the unlocking script. But the nodes need to verify this. We will look at how nodes verify the five types of scripts

First, we will look at the basic script which is the **Pay to PubKey P2PK**

To execute a locking script in P2PK an OP code called **CHECKSIG** is used.

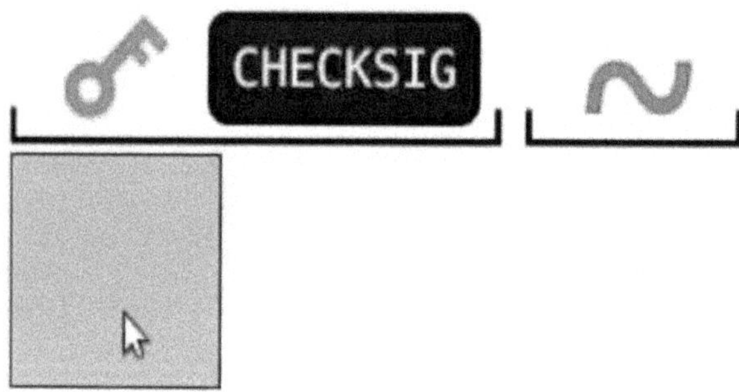

To verify this, node displaces the signature from the end to the beginning.

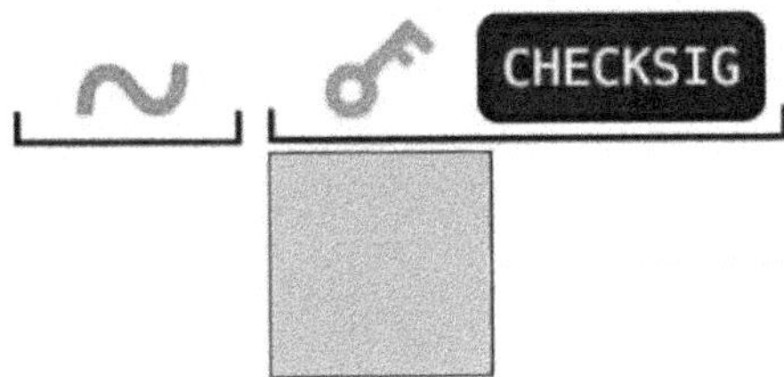

Bitcoin script is a stacked based programming language. If you have basic computer science knowledge you might be knowing what a stack is.

For others, consider stack as a CD rack in which First to get in is the Last to get Out. In C.S it is called LIFO or Last in First Out. We can also displace elements inside the stack, meaning pull out elements from the stack, execute an action and push it back into stack.

Check out the image on the next page.

Here is you boy Stack!!!

A node stacks each element from the locking script into the stack one by one

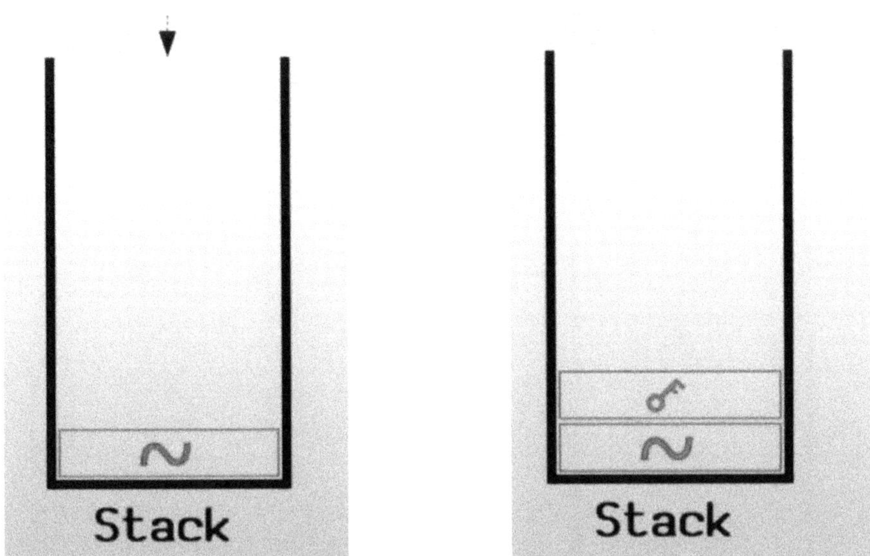

Now we have CHECKSIG left in the script

it pulls out elements of the stack and as the name suggests it verifies the signature. We already know how signatures are verified using Elliptic curves.

If the signature is valid, it gives the elements in the stack a value of 1 and if invalid gives 0. And the node verifies the transaction.

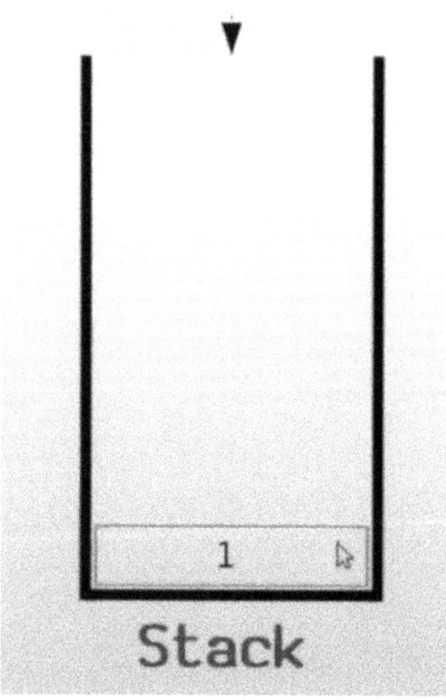

Next in line is **Pay to Public Key Hash or P2PKH**. In this script we hash the public key instead of using it directly in the script to reduce size. What is the hashed version of the public key?

The bloody wallet address!

However, we need multiple OP codes for this OP_DUP, OP_HASH160, OP_EQUALVERIFY, OP_CHECKSIG.

The pictorial representation is in the next page.

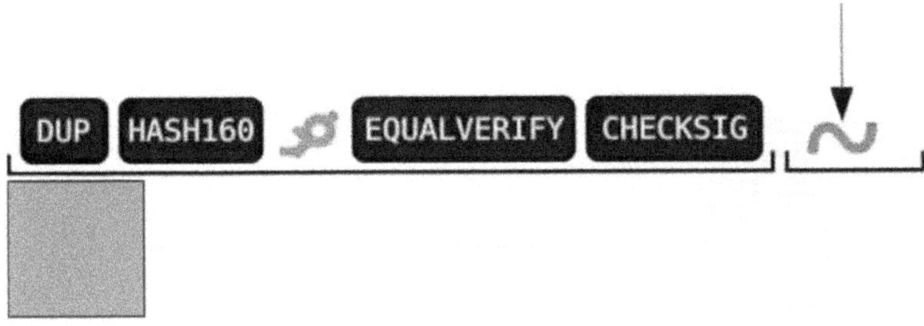

A node rearranges the unlocking script to the left.

Now we need to use stack to verify the transaction. For that we push all elements to the stack. First the unlocking script and then the OP codes are run in the same order as above.

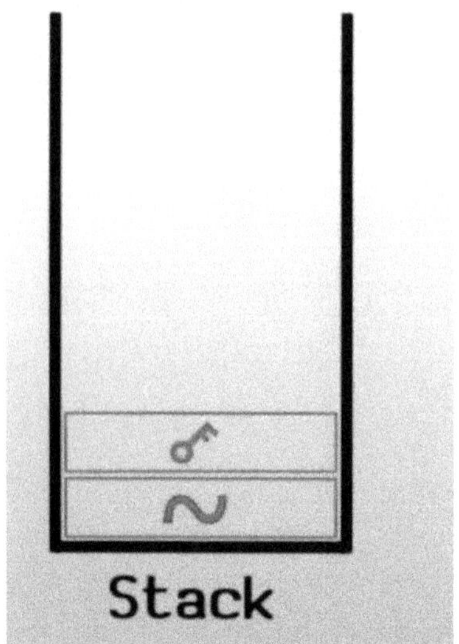

Now the OP_DUP runs. DUP pops the top element in the stack and duplicates it. Here, the top element is the public key. We now have a duplicate or a copy of the public key.

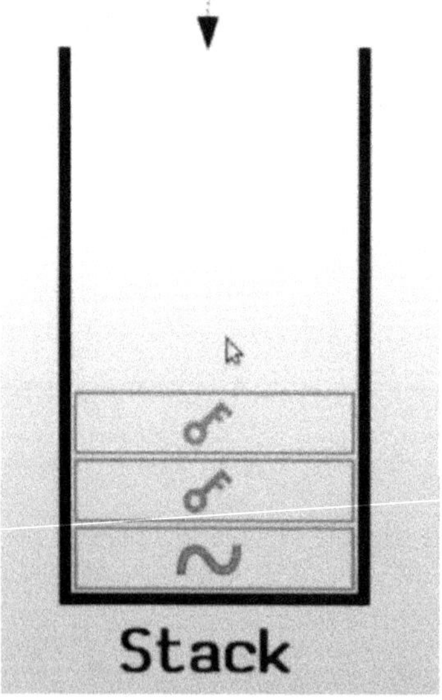

Next in line is the operator OP_HASH160. Hash160 pops the top element from the stack and hashes it.

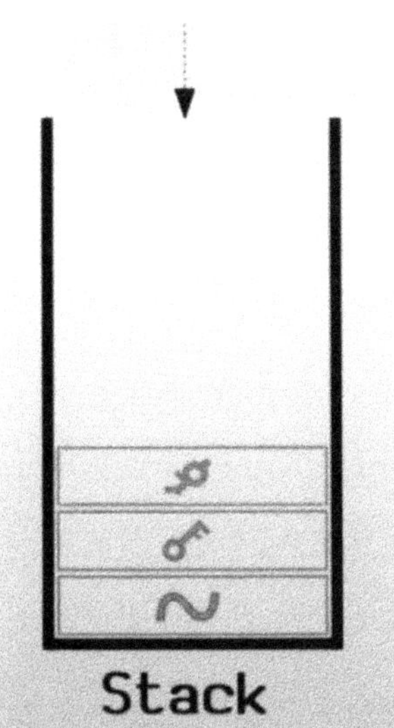

Next, we have the hash of the public key. Let us push into the stack.

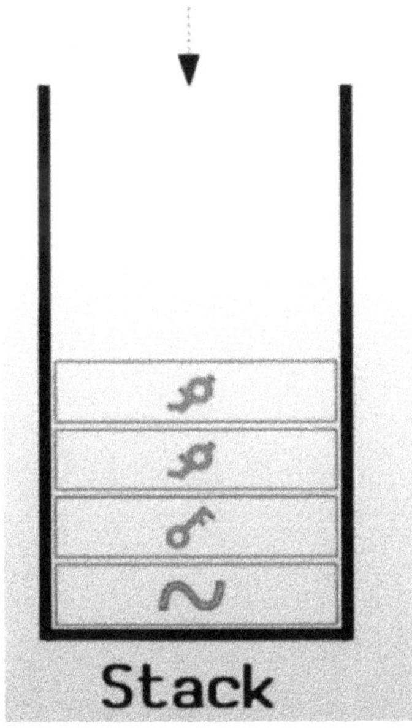

Next OP_EQUALVERIFY runs. EQUALVERIFY checks whether both hashes are the same or not.

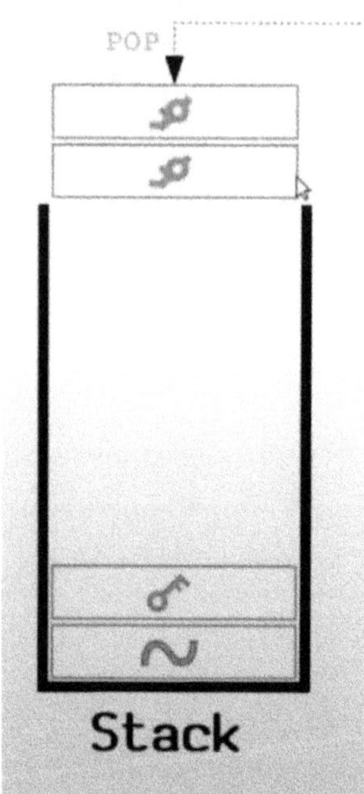

If the hash value is the same, it does not push anything into the stack. Now, only OP_CHECKSIG is left and in the stack, we have the unlocking script element (Public key and Signature). It pops the signature and public key and validates it. If yes, a value of 1 is given to the stack.

But how does the node know if it is P2PK or P2PKH? To make it easier, in a P2PKH hash the wallet address start with the number 1. A node seeing 1 in the front understands that you need to lock the bitcoin using P2PKH.

Next in line is **Pay to Multisig**. Multisig as the name suggests, is a signature created by two or more keys, here we take an example of three keys.

This is how a Multisig script looks like.

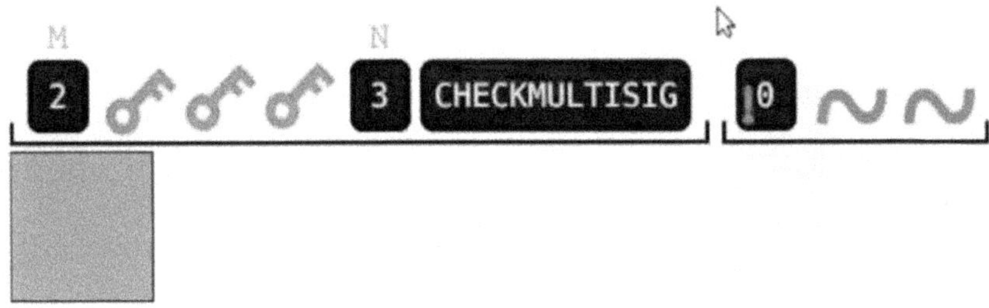

We have few new OP codes here.

- M which has the value of 2 means that 2 signatures are required to verify a multisignature Tx with 3 keys.
- N which has the value 3 means there are three keys involved
- OP_CHECKMULTISIG is the OP code.
- In the unlocking script we have 0 and two signatures. A bug in bitcoin causes M to pop an extra element from the stack. Here M is 2 so because of the bug it will pop out 3 elements. So, zero is given as an element which has no particular value for M to pop out of the stack.
- 2 signatures must be in correct order. We will talk about its significance later.

Verification is similar to P2PK and P2PKH, unlocking script to the left.

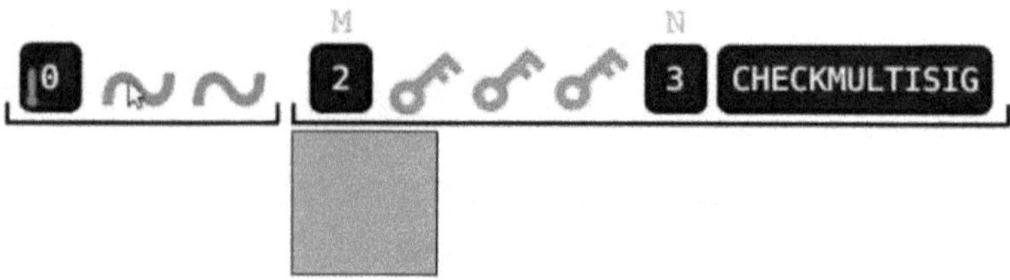

As usual unlocking script goes into the stack first. Numbers go into the stack as data. Let us fill the stack.

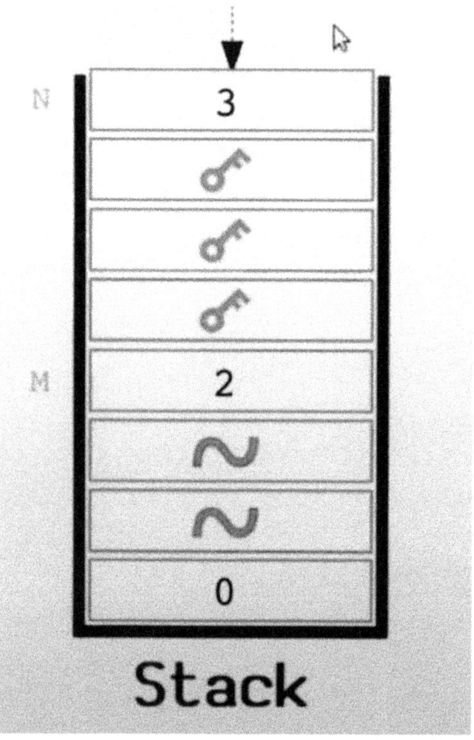

Now only the OP code remains.

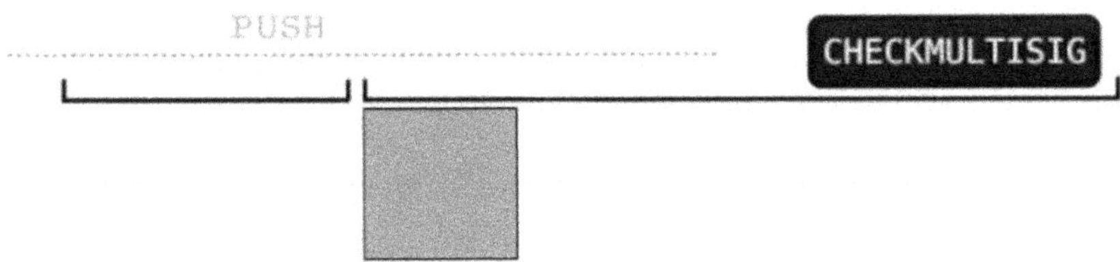

When OP_CHECKMULTISIG is run it pops the top element out of the stack.

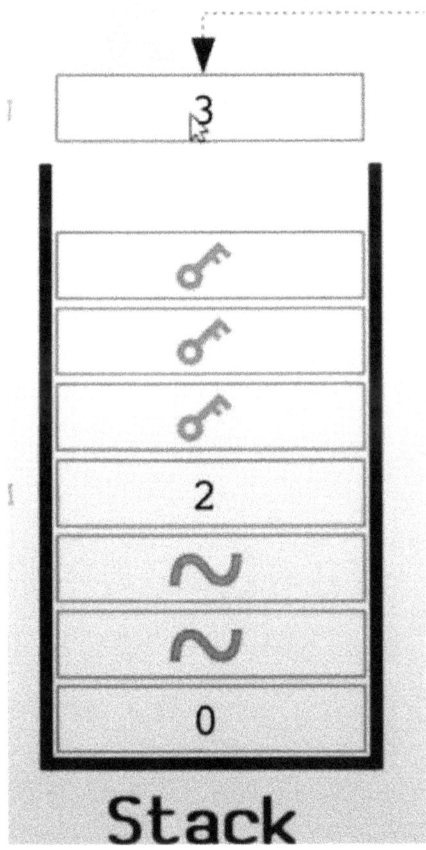

3 will pop out the next three elements from the stack and 2 will pop out next 2 elements but due to the bug it will pop zero as well.

Zero is there so we are never bothered about the bug.

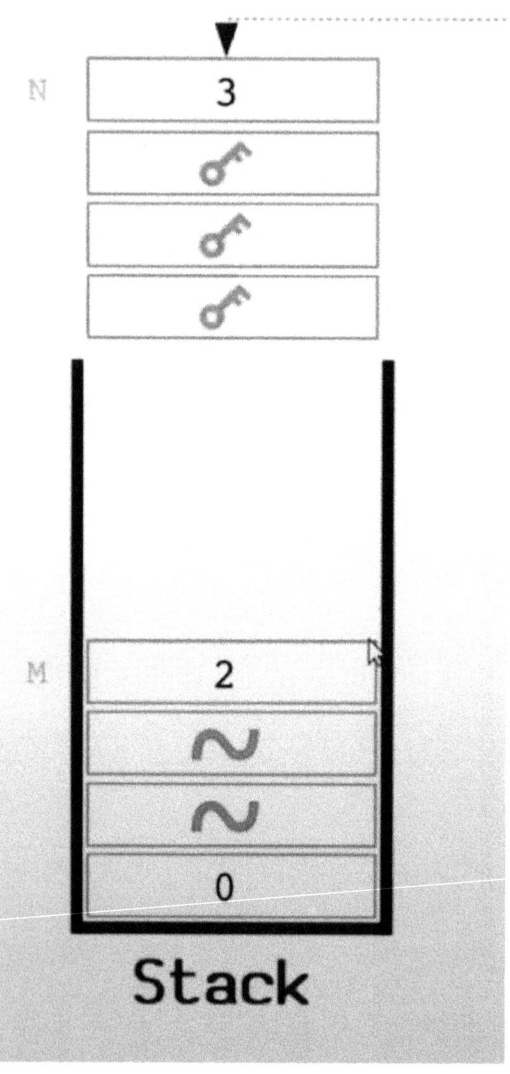

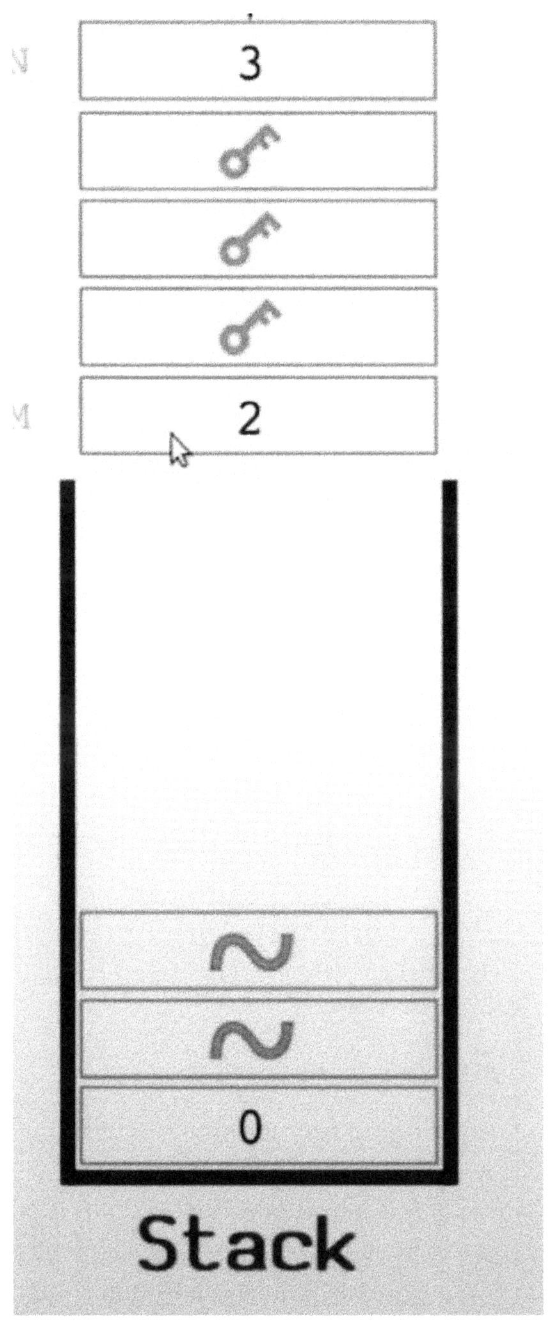
Stack

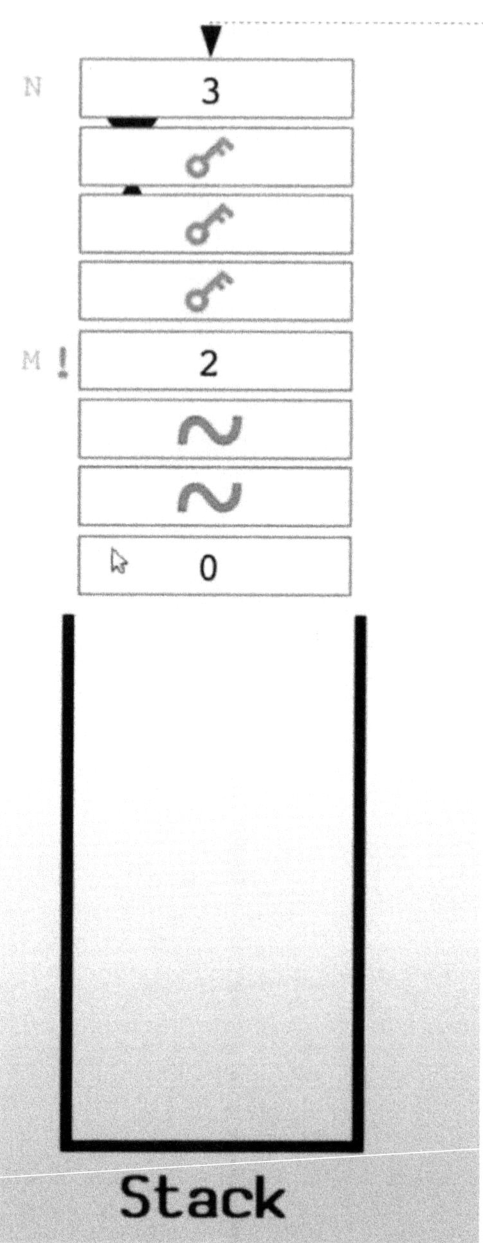

N
3
M
2
0
Stack

To verify the signatures, the OP code will check the public key in sequence. It checks the first public key against the first signature and say it does not match. The second key is checked and the second public key matches.

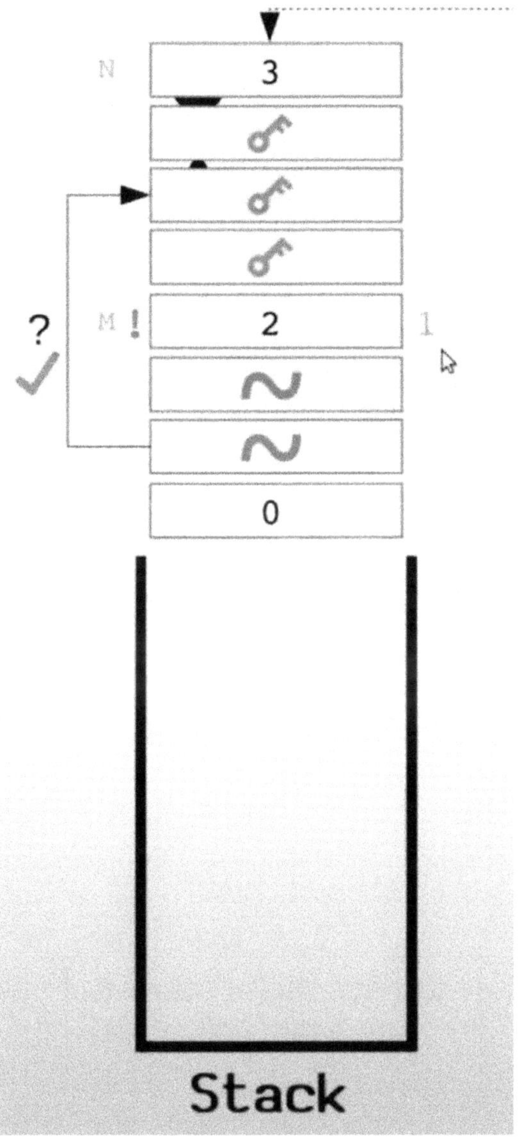

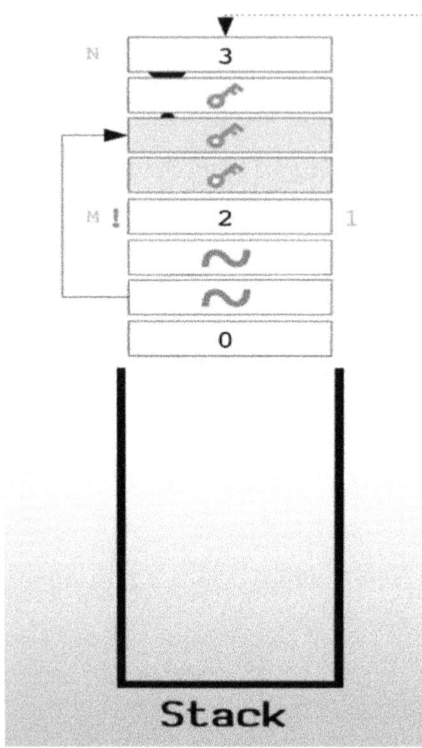

In the beginning we said the signatures must be in the correct sequence. That is because once a key does not match the first signature it will not be considered again for the second signature. So, if the first two keys do not match the first signature, and when the second signature is checked it will not consider 1&2 as it is already discarded. But the second signature's key must be either 1 or 2 right. However, it will not matter unfortunately, and the verification will fail.

Now the second signature is checked and the third key is only considered. If its valid both signatures are now verified.

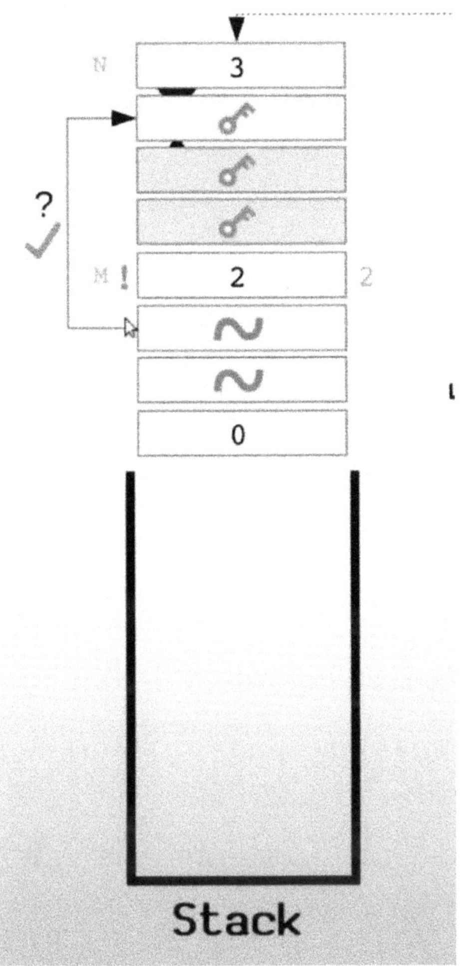

After verification of the signatures a value 1 is pushed into the stack. And the node verification is complete.

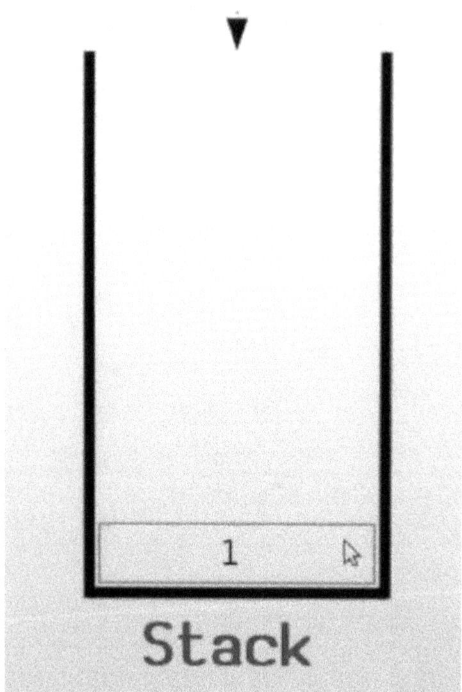

Next in line is **Pay to Script Hash or P2SH**

One of the reasons we need P2SH is due to the size of a Multisig Tx. The above Tx script is 105 bytes in memory. In a Multisig Tx the number of keys is directly proportional to the size of the Tx. More the number of keys larger is the size.

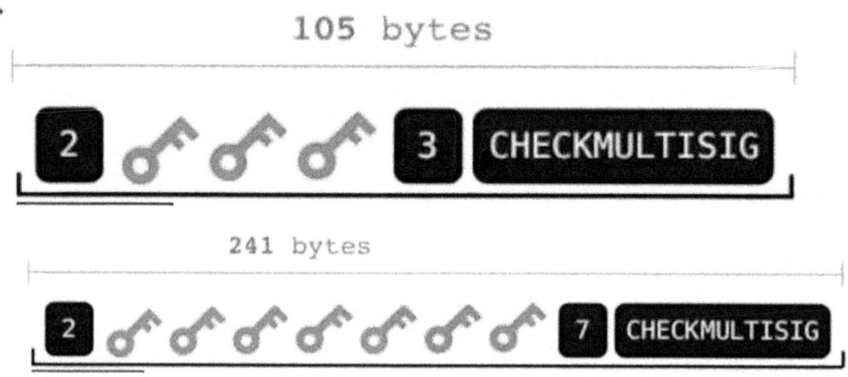

A 7 key Tx will have a size of 241 bytes. This is mainly because every public key takes 33 bytes of space.

So, to reduce Tx size we use P2SH script. P2SH was later implemented as an upgrade to bitcoin. We will talk about upgrades in their own respective dedicated chapters.

Coming back, in P2SH we take the whole locking script

And hashes and wraps it between OP codes HASG160 and EQUAL. This hash is called the **Pay to Script Hash.**

Pay To Script Hash

OP_HASH160 <Scripthash> OP_EQUAL is the Pay to Script Hash.

The locking and unlocking script looks like this.

However, in the unlocking script 2, the public keys, 3 and CHECKMULTISIG are added together as data and not individual codes.

The node verification is same as before.

Now we need to fill the stack.

In P2SH a copy of the stack is made.

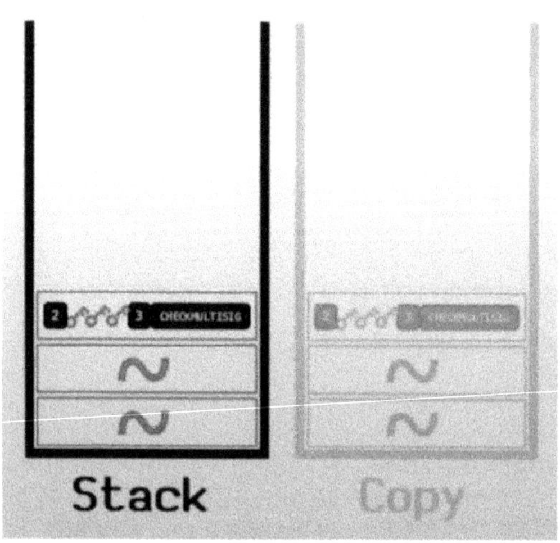

We will get back to the copied stack's role.

Now we need to run the OP codes.

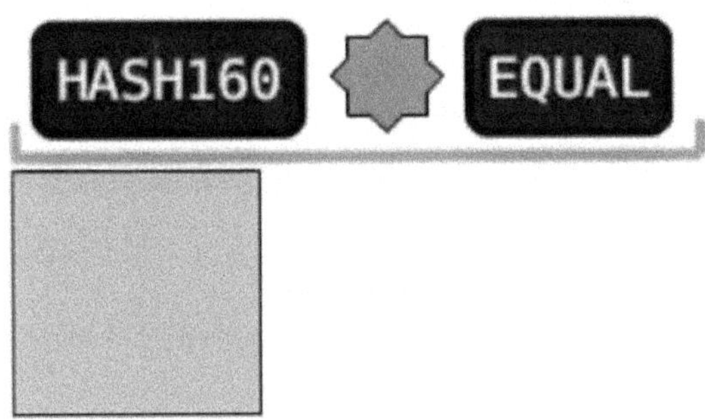

HASH160 pops the top element and hashes it.

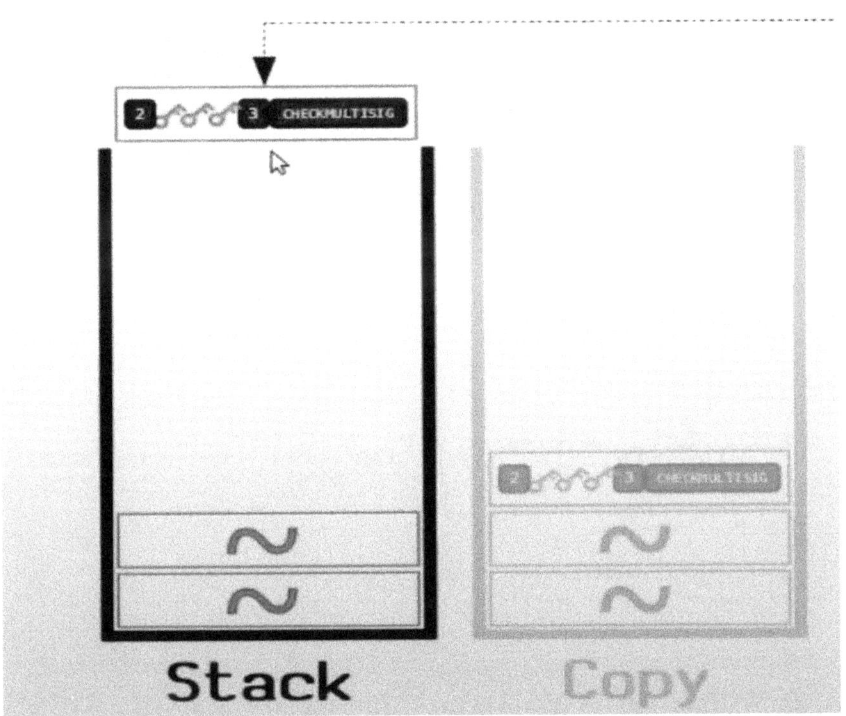

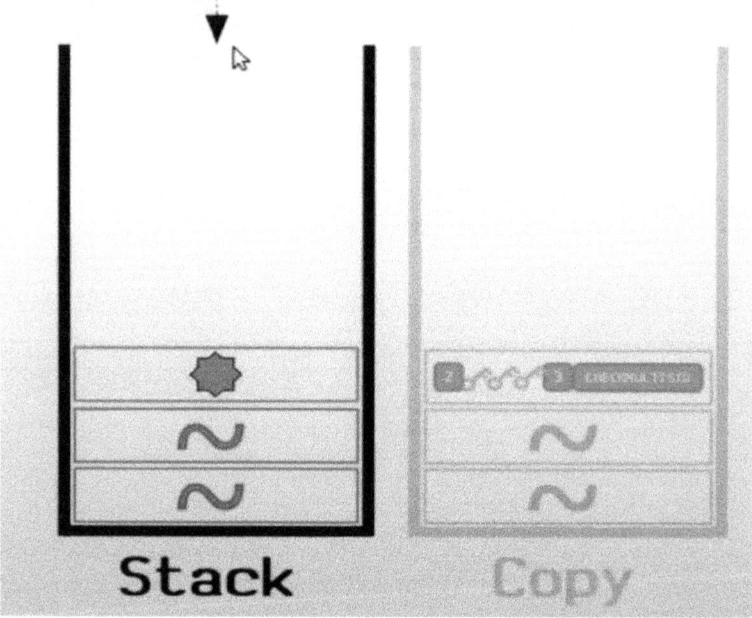

Now we have the remaining script.

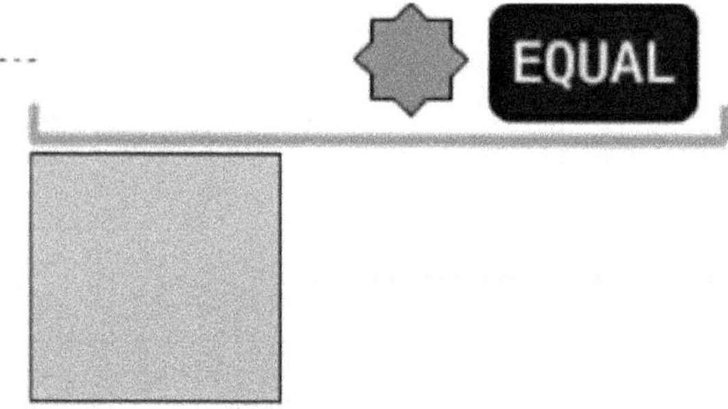

The hash goes into the stack leaving EQUAL in the script.

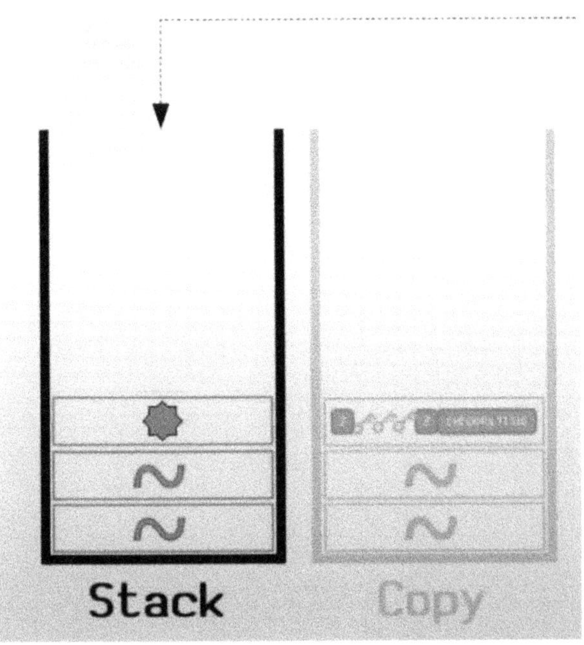

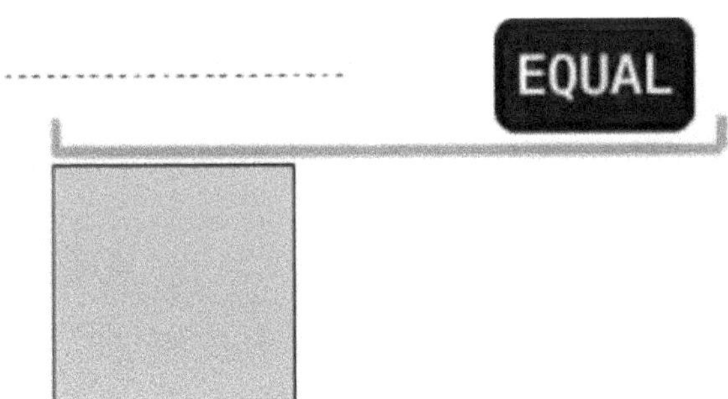

The OP code EQUAL pops the two top elements and check whether they are equal or not. If equal a value of 1 is pushed into the stack.

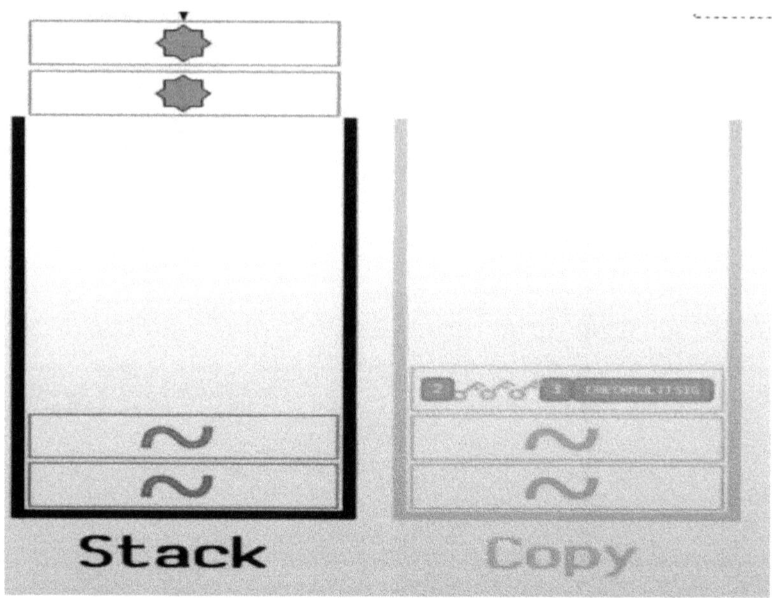

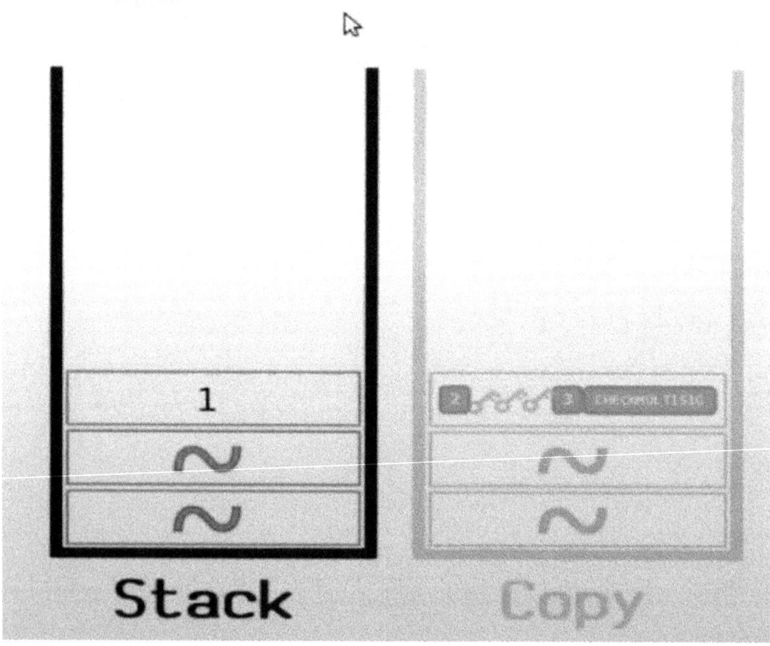

Now the copy of the stack is taken into consideration.

The top element is popped out and added in the script.

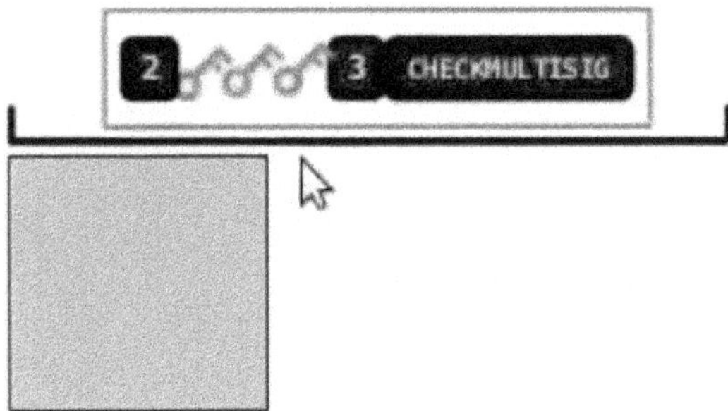

This code is entered into the stack as individual codes rather than as a data.

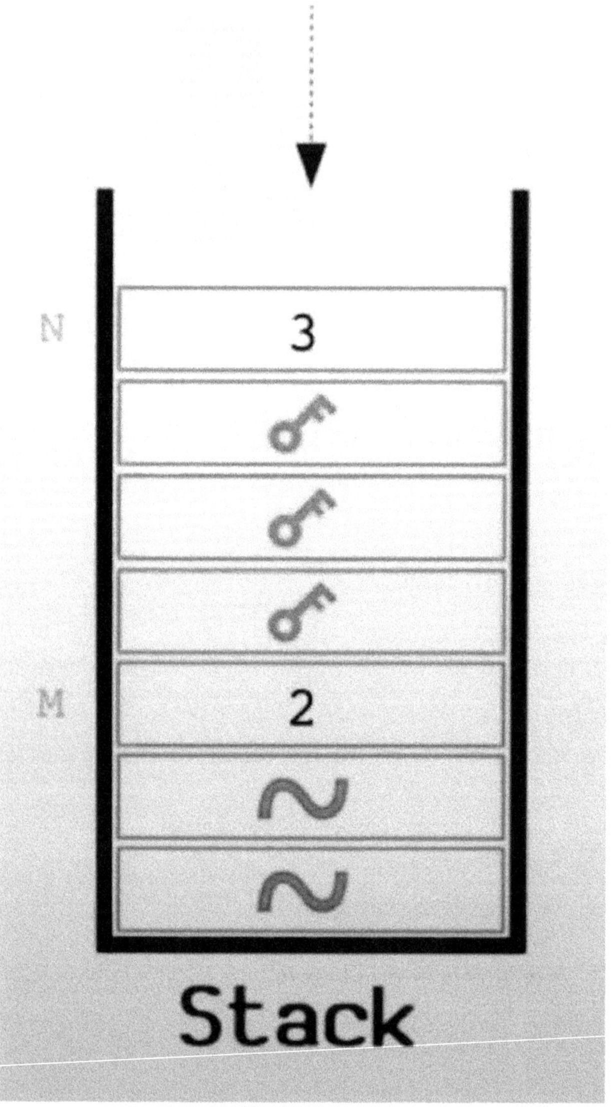

Now the OP code CHECKMULTISIG is run.

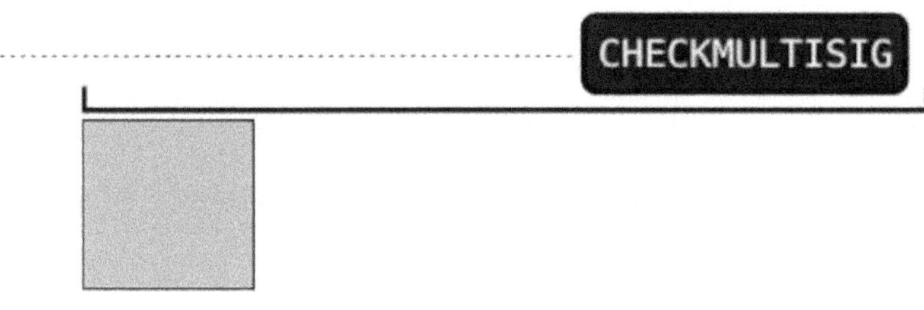

Similar to P2MS, it pops all elements and verifies both signature against the three public keys and if they match a value of 1 is pushed into the stack verifying the transaction.

Remember to come back to this chapter when we talk about upgrades like SegWit and Native SegWit.

The last script we are going to talk about is **Return.**

The OP code RETURN invalidates any script. No matter what you put in a stack the RETURN code invalidates it.

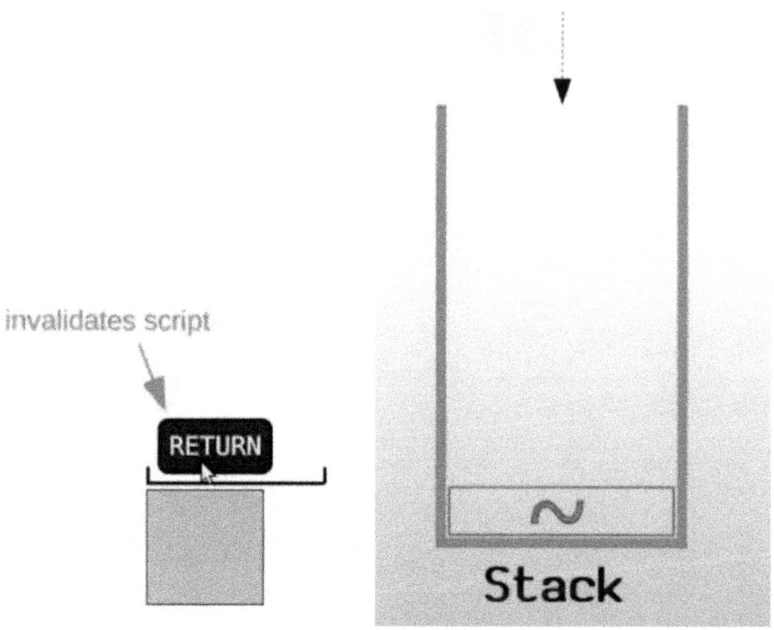

This is used to create a dummy Tx to add a data to it, for example will you marry.

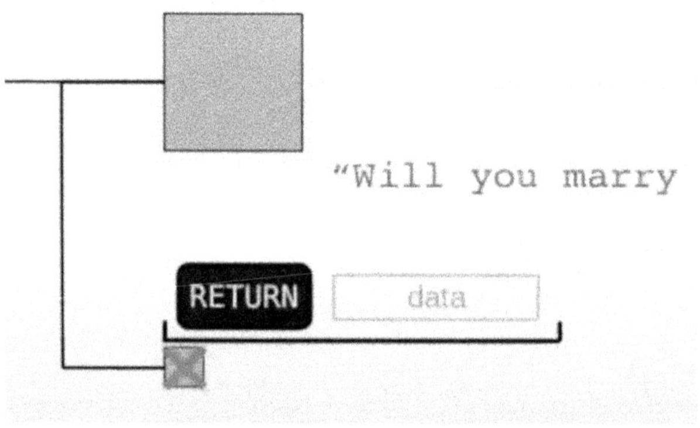

We have other OP codes as well

- ADD

- SUB
- IF
- ELSE
- SHA256
- RIPEMD160
- And numbers from 0-16

From this code we can create scripts like ADD 8 EQUAL as the locking script and if the unlocking script is 6 2. As we know 6 2 goes into the stack first. The OP code ADD is run and 6+2 is 8. 8 is returned to the stack and then EQUAL is run. The value is 8 so you are eligible to unlock and spent the bitcoin.

However, a node will not accept a non-standard script. Only way to add it is by mining the block ourselves. This is not allowed primarily because there are a wide variety of OP codes where all of the code combinations are not tested for vulnerabilities.

A combination of OP code may be used to attack the network like a code which makes verification calculation long can attack the integrity of the network. That is why Bitcoin Script is not turing complete.

Satoshi developed the Bitcoin Script and all other ingredients were there. Only thing he did was he took all the ingredients cleaned them well and prepared a wonderful meal for us to enjoy.

I hope you guys are awake! and congratulations if you have made it this far. Now we have the recipe let us prepare the dish for one last time.

Chapter 18

Bitcoin: A comprehensive overview of the technology behind the world's first Cryptocurrency.

The grand dad, the undisputed king, the first cryptocurrency, a coded marvel and the list goes on!! Bitcoin truly revolutionized the way we perceive money. We have a complex set of technologies working together to maintain the network. This harmony fosters security, decentralization, trust and transparency.

In this chapter we bring all of them to one destination and talk about Bitcoin as a whole offering a holistic view of how Bitcoin works. People who are bored of summaries feel free to skip this chapter. Others can enjoy the song!!!

Blockchain is the heart of Bitcoin. The distributed ledger which keeps all the transaction data in a secure and immutable way. Blockchain is a series of blocks with transaction data in each connected as a chain where each of the blocks are linked to the previous one using cryptographic hashing, hence the name Blockchain.

Blockchain is decentralized, immutable and transparent. In simple words, no single authority controls the network, once a data is recorded it cannot be altered without consensus, and all participants can verify the data on chain at any time.

Every computer on the bitcoin network is called a 'Node'. The moment the ledger is filled and locked in a block a copy of this ledger is sent to all the nodes. Each and every node keeps the whole copy of the blockchain in their computers. So long story short DLT refers to a digital system for recording transactions across multiple locations simultaneously, eliminating the need for a central authority. But we need to incentivize nodes who run computers 24/7.

For that, once a computer fills a ledger and creates a block, that particular computer can add one more transaction to the ledger called the "Coinbase transaction". This transaction in particular will have that person's wallet address claiming for a payment for the work he has done. We cannot pay in fiat currency, right? That would fail the sole purpose for which bitcoin was created in the first place. Instead of that the block creator gets the reward in bitcoins. This is called 'Block Reward'.

In 2009 when the protocol kickstarted the block reward was 50 BTC per block. That means a computer who creates a block will receive 50 BTC as reward. This is the only way bitcoin comes into existence. Nobody else can create bitcoin other than the block creators.

But this poses a serious issue. On an average it takes around 10 mins to create one block on the bitcoin blockchain. That means every 10 mins 50BTC comes into existence. If you do the math, it will be 300 BTC in an hour and 7200 BTC in one day. This means bitcoin will forever print money at a rate of 7200 units per day.

To prevent this once every 210,000 blocks the block reward is cut into half. This is called the infamous 'Bitcoin Halving'.10 min block time means this usually takes around 4 years. We have had four halving events since the inception of BTC.

- Nov. 28, 2012, to 25 bitcoins
- July 9, 2016, to 12.5 bitcoins
- May 11, 2020, to 6.25 bitcoins
- April 19, 2024, to 3.125 bitcoins

Every bitcoin on the blockchain have originated from a Coinbase Tx. We talked about PoW, ECDSA, UTXO and Bitcoin Script earlier. And we know for the fact that the easiest part is taking a transaction from the "mempool" and hashing it using SHA256. But in order to receive the block reward a miner has to solve a cryptographic puzzle as well. All unconfirmed Txs in a mempool are placed there by nodes. Unfortunately, only miners are incentivized for the work, nodes verify Tx and keeps a copy of blockchain for security.

A miner finds the PoW for the candidate block using NONCE and the Difficulty Target and broadcasts it to the network. Every Node can verify the proof of work thus solving the Byzantine Generals Problem. The miner adds fees of all Tx in the block plus the block reward into the coinbase transaction.

To store this bitcoin, we need wallets. Private and Public keys and Digital Signatures are based on ECDSA. And never share the private key with anyone. Private key is a random number and the public key is derived from private key using elliptic curves. A bitcoin address is a double hash of the public key using SHA 256 and RIPEMD160.

When we mix all the concepts into a software called "Bitcoin", the blocks maintain a list of UTXOs. Each UTXO is like a batch of bitcoin and the correct technical term is "output" of each transaction. Whenever a transaction is executed on the network, the wallet owner unlocks the bitcoin using his private key with the help of Bitcoin script, enters the address of the recipient and adds a new locking script into the bitcoin.

A part of the input is sent back to the owner if the input is less than the UTXO. Fees are not part of the UTXO list. Once the Tx is mined onto the blocks, the UTXO is updated and broadcasted to every node creating an updated list of outputs in the network or unspent outputs of the network.

When the recipient needs to spent the coins, first he unlocks the locking code using his private key, enters the address or public key of the next receiver and adds a new locking code using bitcoin script.

That is Bitcoin for you a ledger of locked unspent transaction outputs!!!!

Chapter 19

Key Figures in Bitcoin: The Pioneers and innovators Behind the Cryptocurrency Revolution

Satoshi Nakamoto approached key cryptographers and computer scientist to get assistance in coding Bitcoin. While Bitcoin's Road to success was paved by a multitude of factors, key figures have played a crucial role in shaping Bitcoin's development and success. From its mysterious creator to the early devs, the miners, the baton holders such as Michael Saylor and Max Keiser, each individual and group has built the foundation for Bitcoin.

In this chapter we will talk about the key figures who contributed to Bitcoin's success. These individuals helped transform Bitcoin from an obscure idea to a widely adopted cryptocurrency.

Satoshi Nakamoto: The Mysterious Creator

Satoshi Nakamoto the most enigmatic figure, the creator of Bitcoin. Satoshi Nakamoto is the person/group who have developed the Bitcoin protocol and released the whitepaper in 2008.

Satoshi conceptualized and developed the Bitcoin core and protocol. Satoshi mined the Genesis Block on January 3rd 2009. Despite being the godfather figure, satoshi vanished from the public eye in 2010. He left without leading any concrete information about their identity. The world tried to find satoshi in potential candidates but failed to uncover the mystery. Even though he left, his vision and work has surely inspired every crypto evangelist out there. His work was carried by others and laid the foundation for the crypto world we see today.

Hal Finney: The First Bitcoin Developer and Recipient

Hal Finney was a well-respected cryptographer and computer scientist. He was one of the first people approached by Satoshi to code Bitcoin. Hal was the first person apart from Satoshi to run the Bitcoin client software and receive the first ever Bitcoin transaction of 10BTC. He was actively involved in the early developments of Bitcoin.

Finney improved the Bitcoin codebase. He was a strong advocate of Bitcoin and worked hard to improve its code and spread its adoption. Hal Finney also worked for PGP (Pretty Good Privacy) encryption. He also stipulated RPOW or Reusable Proof of works a system resembling Bitcoin. Unfortunately, Hal Finney passed away in August of 2014 due to ALS. His body is cryopreserved in the Alcor Life Extension Foundation.

Gavin Andresen: Bitcoin's Lead Developer

After Satoshi, Gavin Andresen is the next best man when it comes to Bitcoin development. Andresen was selected by Satoshi as the lead dev for bitcoin when he decided to leave Bitcoin and his community presence. Andresen founded the Bitcoin Foundation in 2012 which fought most of the legal battles faced by Bitcoin.

Gavin proposed an increase in the block size via hard forking Bitcoin to BitcoinXT. This was never accepted by the miners and never reached the required 75% consensus. Gavin Andresen grew the Bitcoin developer community and took care of the coding process in Satoshi's absence. He later stepped down as the lead developer to concentrate on promoting Bitcoin. His hard work is still praised by many Bitcoin enthusiasts till date and his contribution as a developer was valuable for the growth of Bitcoin.

Nick Szabo: A Visionary Cryptographer

Nick Szabo is a cryptographer who proposed the idea of a digital currency way before Bitcoin. Although he was not directly linked to the development of bitcoin, his contributions to the concepts of smart contracts and cryptocurrencies were crucial.

He proposed the idea of a digital currency through a prototype called Bit Gold in late 1990s which was very similar to Bitcoin. It used proof of work systems and was much of a precursor to the idea of blockchain based currency.

Szabo is also infamous for spreading the word on smart contracts. These found its way to Ethereum and it is the very definition of Ethereum now. Szabo also wrote papers on money and was an advocate for decentralized, trustless and inflation resistant form of money.

Adam Back: The creator of HashCash

Adam back is best known for his company called Blockstream which aims to settle bitcoin transactions off chain and also for the development of HashCash. Adam Back is also considered to be Satoshi by many people in the crypto space. His HashCash used proof of work system to prevent email spam and Denial of Service (Ddos attacks). It is the same POW system used by bitcoin as its consensus mechanism.

Adam was one of the early advocates of Bitcoin. He corresponded with Satoshi in the early days and was mentioned in the whitepaper. He even used to edit Bitcoin articles and pages on Wikipedia.

He is the Co-founder and CEO of Blockstream. He is now working on a concept called Liquid Bitcoin which is a sidechain for Bitcoin transactions. Adam Back is also part of **COPA Crypto Open Patent Alliance** which fought in court against Craig Wright who claimed to be Satoshi Nakamoto and demanded copyright right for bitcoin.

Martti Malmi: Bitcoin's Designer

Martti Malmi is a Finnish software developer and was one among the developers who worked with Satoshi. He wrote parts of the code, did bug fixes and designed web pages under the instructions of Satoshi himself.

Malmi was the person who suggested to start a Bitcoin exchange for mass adoption and recognition. The name of the exchange was BitcoinMarket.com. This marked the first real world price discovery for Bitcoin. It began operation in March 2010 and the first recorded price was 1000 BTC for 1$.

Malmi was also part of COPA and testified in court. His email conversations with Satoshi have been made private and is accessible to public on GitHub.

Malmi was an active developer in the early stages of Bitcoin. He also provided guidance and support to the early crypto community. He tested most of the upgrades made by satoshi and posted it on the Bitcoin forum.

As bitcoin grew Malmi took a step back from active development. But his early work paved the way for the matured community we see today.

Peter Todd: Bitcoin Developer and Researcher

Peter Todd is a famous Bitcoin developer and researcher who immensely contributed to scale Bitcoin. He coded for improving the privacy and security of the network. Peter was one among the main proponents of SegWit (Segregated witness), a protocol upgrade which addressed the block size conflict in the bitcoin community. He concentrates and researches into Bitcoin's security, particularly regarding long term scalability and how to protect bitcoin from vulnerabilities or attacks.

Peter Wuille: BIP master

Peter discovered the orange pill in 2010 and joined the Bitcoin Core development team in May 2011. Peter was behind Various Bitcoin Improvement Proposals BIP 30, 32, 42 and 62 and he also authored libsecp256k1 which contained the efficient use of elliptical curve cryptography for use in Bitcoin.

He works for Blockstream and was previously employed in google. Peter is now only behind fellow Bitcoin core dev, **Vladmir van der Laan**, with a whopping 650 commits on GitHub to the Bitcoin Code.

Roger Ver: Bitcoin Jesus

Roger Ver was the first investor in Bitcoin related projects. He is referred to as the "Bitcoin Jesus". His company **Memory dealers** were the first company to accept Bitcoin as a payment in 2011. Roger also is the founder of **Bitcoinstore.com, Bitcoinbountyhunter.com** a website which offers bounty for catching cyber criminals in the Bitcoin space.

Roger was one of the early people who recognized the potential of Bitcoin and adopted the currency.

Andreas M. Antonopoulos: The Bitcoin Evangelist

Antonop is an author and early advocate of bitcoin and is known for his ability to explain the complex structure of Bitcoin to common people. He is the author of many books related to Bitcoin such as **Mastering Bitcoin, The Internet of Money, Bitcoin and Blockchain** etc.

Antonop is a household voice in the crypto space hosting podcast named **Let's talk Bitcoin**. He emphasizes on the philosophical aspects of Bitcoin, such as its potential to empower individuals and financial freedom. Over the course of years, he has surely become one of the most trusted and influential voice in the space.

Satoshi did create Bitcoin but it was these guys and numerous developers who supported and promoted and made it the giant we see today.

Chapter 20

Different Types of Consensus Mechanism

We talked about consensus in Chapter 8. We only talked about Proof of Work consensus in that chapter. Since the inception of Bitcoin there have been numerous developers creating consensus mechanisms. Today we see a multitude of projects with cutting edge consensus mechanism.

Although we cannot go deeper into each and every consensus protocol out there but we sure can dedicate a chapter to summarize them.

As we all know consensus is crucial in any cryptocurrency to solve the Byzantine General Problem. We will be listing and summarizing 10 such consensus protocol in this chapter. Let's get right into it!

Proof of work

Ah the good old proof of work. I thought about skipping pow for this section but was tempted to write about it again. I apologize in advance for writing it again.

POW powers Bitcoin and many other cryptocurrencies. It requires miners to solve the infamous cryptographic puzzle to receive reward for validating blocks. The first miner to solve the puzzle receives the reward and has the right to add the new block on the blockchain.

To make it a level playing field the difficulty is adjusted accordingly when the Hashrate of the network increases or decreases.

POW is highly secure and resistant to **sybil attacks** (fake nodes). It is one of the most decentralized consensus protocols where anyone with computational power can participate.

Example: Bitcoin, Litecoin, Dogecoin

Proof of Stake

Proof of stake is an alternate to Proof of Work that aims to reduce the energy consumption problem with POW systems. Instead of miners POS has validators.

Validators create new blocks and they are selected on the number of tokens they hold and are willing to "Stake" as collateral. It is like being a stakeholder in the company. You need to have a stake in the company to vote or to be a part of the decision-making panel.

So more the tokens staked higher the chance of being a validator. Similar to POW validators are rewarded with Tx fees and newly minted coins. If a validator behaves maliciously or attempts an attack they lose a part of their stake. This type of punishment for bad conduct is called **'slashing'.**

One of the main advantages of PoS is low energy consumption. The tokens locked or staked by network participants reduces the sell pressure of the coin and promotes long term investment on the project. The downside is that there is no difficulty adjustment type of rule in PoS. Richer participants who have more stake has a higher chance of being selected as the validator.

Example: Ethereum 2.0, Cardano, Near Protocol, BNB

Delegated Proof of Stake (DPoS)

DPoS is a variation of the PoS system. Here token holders vote for a small group of **delegators** or validators who are responsible for validating transaction and creation of blocks.

Token holders vote for delegators based on their reputation and performance. The delegators must act honestly. Otherwise, they will be voted out. Well performed and honest delegators are incentivized.

Think about DPoS as appointing a small group of class leaders whose duty is to maintain class decorum. A group of teachers appoints these leaders for a time period. That is where the drawback is. The power is within the hands of those few leaders which can cause centralization. Only benefit is Block creation is faster as there are only few validators.

Example: EOS, TRON

Practical Byzantine Fault Tolerance (PBFT)

Practical Byzantine Fault Tolerance (PBFT) is designed to tackle the Byzantine Faults (malicious actor or faulty nodes) to ensure consensus in a distributed system. Consensus is achieved in PBFT even when some nodes act maliciously, provided that at least two thirds of the participants are honest.

In PDFT, a set of chosen validators participate in a round of consensus. These validators communicate with each other multiple times or rounds to validate transactions. Each validator send message to other to reach an agreement. Consensus is reached when two third of the validatory act honestly.

PDFT is highly efficient than PoW and PoS and its main feature is its tolerance to faulty nodes.

Example: Zilliqa, Hyperledger

Proof of Authority (PoA)

Proof of Authority is used in private or permissioned blockchains generally. In PoA a set of trusted validators based on their identity and reputation have the right to validate transactions and create blocks.

Validators are pre-approved and must be known entities. They maybe individuals, corporations or organizations. Validators takes turn in validation process and their reputation is on the line. Similar to any other consensus validators are rewarded with Tx fees and reward.

However, PoA is not suited for the crypto space as we promote decentralized systems rather than centralized ones. We were eating centralized systems for breakfast lunch and dinner!! Who doesn't like a change?

Example: VeChain

Proof of Space (PoSpace) or Proof of Capacity (PoC)

Proof of Space also known as Proof of Capacity as the name suggests uses the unused hard drive space instead of computational power to attain consensus. In this protocol, miners allocate their hard drives to store cryptographic proofs that can be utilized later to win the right to create blocks.

Here Miners "Farm" space with the help of hard drives, creating a large number of cryptographic "plots". To create blocks miners, check their plots to find out whether it meets the new block requirements. Here more the storage higher the chance of winning.

PoC is less energy hungry when compared to PoW but storage space does not come by easily as computational power.

Example: Chia, Storj.

Proof of Elapsed Time (PoET)

Proof of Elapsed Time (PoET) is consensus mechanism developed by Intel for permissioned blockchains. To ensure the process of waiting for a random amount of time is fair and tamper resistant it relies on a secure hardware called Intel SGX.

After waiting for a certain period of time, validators are randomly selected to validate transactions and create blocks. The secure hardware generates the wait time and is verifiable by the network. Once the wait is over, the chosen node can create the block.

It is a simple and efficient mechanism for private and consortium blockchains. It is also power efficient due to the lack of computational power requirements. The hardware mentioned above is the main drawback as it is not easily accessible.

Proof of Burn (PoB)

Proof of Burn (PoB) is a consensus mechanism where participants burn a certain number of tokens to prove their loyalty and commitment to the network. Burning is the process of sending tokens to a dead address where the tokens are permanently lost. The burned tokens also reduce the supply which is good for the price action.

This is not an ideal method to choose validators. The more you burn the higher chance of being a validator. But what is the point of wasting tokens for consensus. Anyways, someone one might find an appropriate use for this also. So, we are gonna leave it at that eye for now.

Proof of Stake Time (PoST)

Proof of Stake Time (PoST) combines PoS with a time component. Which means validators are rewarded on the basis of how long they held their tokens in a wallet. The longer you hold, the more you can take part in the consensus process.

Hybrid Proof of Work/ Proof of Stake (PoW/PoS)

Some blockchains uses a hybrid mechanism by combining PoW and PoS. The main objective is to use the security of PoW and the energy efficiency of PoS.

In this hybrid model, PoW is used to determine the integrity of blocks, while PoS is used to validate and confirm transactions. This help achieve a balance between decentralization, security, and efficiency.

Having said that it is very complex to implement and code because of both PoW and PoS. But if implemented it can be massive by leveraging both PoW and PoS. Decred and Horizen are an example of that.

From that we looked at the most common consensus mechanisms. Each mechanism has its strength and weakness and ideal use cases. The final objective is to solve the **Byzantine Generals Problem** in a secure and decentralized way. As the space expand, we can surely expect even more powerful consensus mechanisms coming to fruition. And I will be ready with my next book! Haha!!

Chapter 21

Ethereum

Let us move away from Bitcoin for a bit to talk about the modern crypto landscape as a whole. And there is not a candidate worthier than Ethereum to start with. Ethereum is one of significant projects after Bitcoin which altered the crypto space. Ethereum was Launched in 2015 by Vitalik Buterin. At the surface level it was similar to Bitcoin but it had few quirks which made all the difference in the world.

Ethereum made the Nick Szabo smart contracts dream a reality. It is like an operating system where we can deploy decentralized applications called "Dapps", Decentralized Finance Protocols called "DeFi" which has been giving the traditional finance systems a run for their money.

In this chapter, we will explore the world of Ethereum, its core features and its impact on the world.

First things first, Ethereum has transitioned from a Pow consensus to a PoS mechanism (Proof of Work to Proof Of stake). Ethereum was proposed by Vitalik in 2013. He built Ethereum to do things that Bitcoin couldn't and that's a bold statement!!

Buterin's idea of a blockchain was a system that could execute arbitrary code, enabling devs to create more complex and versatile applications beyond simple financial transactions. And the Ethereum whitepaper outline the very idea; a blockchain that could run Dapps using smart contracts. Smart contracts are self-executing contracts where the terms of agreement are directly written into code.

Ethereum's development began in the early 2014. Vitalik collaborated with notable figures like Gavin Wood, Joseph Lubin and Charles Hoskinson. The project raised a whopping 18 million dollars in a crowd sale in 2014. Ethereum went live on July 30, 2015 with the launch of its first live network named Frontier.

Now we move onto the core features of Ethereum

Smart Contracts

Smart contract defines Ethereum. Ethereum allows devs to write self-executing agreements that automatically execute when the predefine conditions are met. These contracts are run on the Ethereum Virtual Machine (EVM). EVM is responsible for the correct and secure execution of smart contracts across the Ethereum network.

How Smart Contracts work:

Smart contracts are written using Solidity, the primary programming language of Ethereum and then deployed on the

Ethereum blockchain. Smart contracts once executed is immutable and tamper resistant. They can never be altered after deployment, which fosters trust in the contract eliminating the requirement of an intermediary. A deployed contract can perform various actions like transferring tokens, executing financial transactions or trigger other smart contracts, all without human intervention.

A simple example would be creating a smart contract for a bank loan approval. Once the criteria of eligibility are laid down and deployed nobody can alter the contract. If you are eligible for the loan, the contract will release the funds irrespective of your religion, race, job or any other factor for which people get scrutinized unnecessarily even though they were eligible for the loan in the first place.

Ether:

Ether (ETH) is the native currency of the Ethereum network, it serves several purposes within the ecosystem:

- ETH is used to pay for transaction fees and computational services on Ethereum referred commonly as "Gas Fees". Miners (when PoW) and now validators get ETH as reward.
- Like Bitcoin, ETH is also used as a store value, though its primary use is as a fuel for smart contracts and execution of transaction on the network. However,

unlike Bitcoin Ethereum's supply is not capped due to high demand for Dapps and other contracts. ETH is issued at a fixed rate.

Ethereum Virtual Machine (EVM):

The Ethereum Virtual Machine is the runtime environment that process smart contracts and transactions on Ethereum. EVM makes Ethereum "turing complete" meaning that it can execute any computation or program, given enough resources. This is what enables Ethereum to run Dapps. You can consider Ethereum Virtual Machine as Java Virtual Machine for easier understanding.

Decentralized Apps (Dapps)

Smart contracts and EVM brought dapps to the dinner table. Dapps run on the Ethereum blockchain rather than on centralized servers, making them censorship resistant and more secure. Dapps can be anything from DeFi platforms to games to social media platforms and supply chain management systems.

In simpler words dapps are like apps on apple appstore or google playstore but decentralized.

We have talked about the key feature of Ethereum and it is time to discuss Ethereum's transition from Proof of Work to Proof of Stake.

Ethereum 2.0 and the need for Eth 2.0

Even though, Ethereum had great success in the crypto space it faced significant challenges, particularly in terms of scalability and energy efficiency.

Ethereum 2.0 is the upgrade which aims to rectify all of these shortcomings. It transitions Ethereum to a new consensus mechanism, drum roll!!! Proof of Stake!!

Proof of Stake makes it more energy efficient and scalable. We move from miners to validators to create new blocks. To take part you need to stake a modest 32 ether!! Yeah, I know!!

Ethereum 2.0 will also feature "Sharding". Sharding is the process of splitting a blockchain into multiple chains, called "shards" to process transactions parallelly. This dramatically scales the Ethereum network to handle many transactions per second.

The new PoS blockchain is called the "Beacon Chain" and first ran parallel to the existing Ethereum network. The Beacon Chain then merged with Ethereum's PoW chain, fully transitioning Ethereum to PoS consensus.

All updates will be brought out in Phases and not all together to properly test the transition.

When we talk about Ethereum we need to address the whole ecosystem behind Ethereum as well. Most of the tokens on the Ethereum network are known as **ERC-20** tokens. ERC-20 is a standard for Fungible tokens on the Ethereum network. And a fungible token means a token where each unit are the same. For example, Us dollar is fungible as all 1$ bills have the same value. For Non fungible tokens or NFT the standard is ERC-721.

ERC-20 was proposed by dev Fabian Vogelsteller in 2015 and came to force in 2017. For a token to meet the ERC-20 standard it has to fulfill a list of criteria called functions and events. They are:

- Total supply of the token
- The account balance of a token owner's account
- Automatically execute transfers of a specified number of tokens to a specified address using the token.
- Allow a spender to withdraw a set of number of tokens from a specified account, up to a specific amount.
- Returns a set of number of tokens from a spender to the owner.

Ethereum of course is the heart of the ecosystem and it powers the DeFi (decentralized Finance) movement. DeFi aims to create a world with permissionless and open financial system. Major projects in the DeFi space include Uniswap, Aave,

Compound etc. These DeFi platforms bring decentralized exchanges, lending, borrowing and decentralized stablecoins to the Ethereum ecosystem.

I know some of your frothing for the NFT part!!

Ahh! The wild west of crypto Non fungible tokens or NFTs, they are non-fungible (each unit is unique) and it represents ownership of a specific item, it can be digital arts, collectibles, paintings or even real estate for that matter. NFT follow the **ERC 721** standard. The idea of the standard was published as a paper by William Entriken and co-authors Dieter Shirley, Jacob Evans and Nastassia Sachs. Popular NFT marketplace in Ethereum is OpenSea and Rarible.

For your information, there is also a standard called **ERC-1155** which combines the ERC-20 and ERC-721. With this you can create fungible, semi fungible and non-fungible tokens in a single contract. It was proposed by the CTO of Enjin Witek Radomski. Popular ERC-1155 projects are Enjin, Horizen Games, OpenSea etc.

We also have organizations on Ethereum called **Decentralized Autonomous Organization** or **DAO** governed by smart contracts and operate without central control. A DAO can be anything from a community driven governance to investment funds and charities.

Although Ethereum is a powerhouse of a project, it too has shortcomings and drawbacks.

Despite its innovations, Ethereum is hard to scale due to the number of Dapps and users. In peak crypto frenzy the network always gets congested, leading to high transaction fees and slower processing of transactions. Sharding will solve this bottleneck, however, it will take at least a year or two get implemented.

Ethereum is also famous for its high gas fees during peak traffic. I have seen fees as much as 50$ for a transaction! In the current situation small retail investors stay away from Ethereum due to the high gas.

However, we are pulling the trigger very early here, crypto itself is a very fresh market and Ethereum is even younger. We will have to give time for these projects to merge with the real world and to find solutions for the problems we face now. And this space adapts and updates over a fortnight.

Unfortunately, I cannot talk about each and every project out there. But me being your favorite author has to fill your curious mind. So, in the next chapter we will talk about the various types of cryptocurrencies.

Chapter-22

Different types of Cryptocurrencies

There is an ocean of cryptos out there and the water is infested with sharks, whales and even mackerels. Navigation is hard these days but it is your lucky day today! We will categorize cryptos to make your job as an investor hassle free.

I also look at the category of the token I am interested in and this is surely very helpful in clearing the clutter to certain extent. Yeah! A certain extent only.

So, my little crypto minions!! in this chapter, we will explore the different types of cryptocurrencies, categorizing them based on their purpose, technology, and applications. Understanding these categories is crucial for anyone seeking to navigate the world of digital currencies, whether as an investor, developer, or enthusiast.

Altcoins: The Alternatives to Bitcoin

Altcoins, or alternative coins, are any cryptocurrencies other than Bitcoin. They were created to offer solutions to perceived limitations in Bitcoin, such as scalability, transaction speed, and energy consumption. Over time, the altcoin market has grown, and many altcoins have developed unique features and use cases that distinguish them from Bitcoin. Let us look at the most popular ones.

Ethereum (ETH):

Yeahh!! Ethereum is an altcoin. Being the second largest cryptocurrency by market cap, had to mention Ethereum.

Ripple (XRP):

Ripple is a digital payment protocol and cryptocurrency designed for fast and low-cost cross-border transactions. XRP is the native cryptocurrency of the Ripple network. Ripple processes transactions in seconds and is capable of handling thousands of transactions per second. Ripple has partnered with many financial institutions and payment providers. XRP facilitates international remittances and settlement between financial institutions.

Litecoin (LTC):

Litecoin is a peer-to-peer cryptocurrency created by Charlie Lee in 2011. It is based on Bitcoin's code but features faster block generation times and a different hashing algorithm (Scrypt). Litecoin's block time is around 2.5 minutes, compared to Bitcoin's 10 minutes, making it faster for transaction.

Litecoin's lower fees make it an attractive option for microtransactions.

Stablecoins: Cryptocurrencies Pegged to Fiat

Stablecoins are a class of cryptocurrencies designed to maintain a stable value by being pegged to a fiat currency like the US dollar or commodities such as gold. Stablecoins address the volatility issues that are common in many cryptocurrencies, making them more suitable for everyday transactions and as a store of value.

Examples of Popular Stablecoins:

Tether (USDT):

Tether is the most widely used stablecoin, pegged 1:1 to the US dollar. It is primarily used to provide liquidity in cryptocurrency markets. Tether's value is consistently close to one US dollar. Tether is used widely in trading and provides a way for crypto traders to move in and out of the market quickly without converting to fiat currency.

USD Coin (USDC):

USD Coin is another popular stablecoin backed by the US dollar. It is issued by regulated financial institutions and operates on various blockchains, including Ethereum and

Solana. USDC is backed by cash and short-term US government bonds. Regular audits ensure that the USDC supply is fully backed by reserves.

Privacy Coins: Anonymity and Security

Privacy coins are cryptocurrencies designed with privacy and anonymity as their primary focus. These coins use advanced cryptographic techniques to ensure that transactions are untraceable and confidential, providing enhanced security for users who wish to keep their financial activities private.

Examples of Popular Privacy Coins:

Monero (XMR):

Monero is a privacy-focused cryptocurrency that uses ring signatures, stealth addresses, and bulletproofs to ensure transaction privacy. Monero transactions are private by default, and it's nearly impossible to trace the sender, receiver, or amount. Because all transactions are private, Monero is fully fungible, meaning each unit is indistinguishable from another. Monero is used by individuals who value privacy and wish to keep their financial activities confidential.

Zcash (ZEC):

Zcash is another privacy coin that uses zero-knowledge proofs (zk-SNARKs) to allow transactions to be verified without revealing any information about the sender, recipient, or amount. Zcash allows users to choose whether their transactions are private or transparent. Users can send shielded transactions that hide transaction details.

Governance Tokens: Decentralized Decision-Making

Governance tokens are a type of cryptocurrency that provides holders with the ability to participate in the governance and decision-making processes of a blockchain project. These tokens are often used in decentralized autonomous organizations (DAOs) and DeFi protocols, where token holders vote on proposals and changes to the system.

Examples of Popular Governance Tokens:

Maker (MKR):

Maker is the governance token of the MakerDAO platform, which manages the Dai stablecoin. MKR holders vote on important protocol changes, such as collateral types and risk parameters.

MKR token holders have voting power in MakerDAO's governance. MakerDAO allows users to generate the Dai stablecoin by collateralizing assets such as Ethereum. MKR is used to make decisions on how the Maker protocol operates.

Uniswap (UNI):

Uniswap's governance token allows holders to vote on changes to the Uniswap decentralized exchange protocol. UNI token holders participate in the decision-making process for the future of Uniswap.

UNI holders vote on changes to the Uniswap protocol, including fee structures and liquidity pools.

Oracle Tokens:

Oracles act as bridges between the blockchain and external data sources. Blockchains themselves are "closed systems" and do not have access to real-world data, such as stock prices, weather information, or even the outcomes of sports events. Oracles provide these external data feeds to smart contracts, enabling decentralized applications (dApps) to make decisions based on real-world events.

Examples of Popular Oracle Tokens:

Chainlink (LINK):

Chainlink is one of the most widely used decentralized oracle networks, providing secure and reliable off-chain data to smart contracts. The LINK token is the native token of the Chainlink network. Data providers (called *oracle nodes*) are rewarded in LINK tokens for retrieving and verifying data. Users who require data (such as smart contract developers) also pay in LINK tokens to access the oracle services.

Band Protocol (BAND):

Band Protocol is another decentralized oracle network that aggregates real-world data for smart contracts. The BAND token is used for governance, staking, and paying for data requests on the Band Protocol network. Users of the network pay in BAND tokens to request data, and token holders can participate in governance decisions.

API3 (API3):

API3 is a newer oracle platform that focuses on enabling decentralized APIs (dAPIs). The API3 token is used to govern the network and incentivize data providers.

Data providers (API providers) stake API3 tokens to ensure they offer reliable services. The tokens are also used for governance and decision-making on the protocol.

As you saw we have a wide variety of categories and it is growing every day. Sadly, I cannot go in details within the scope of this book. Let me know in the reviews if you need a detailed book on crypto categories. *I am your merciful lord!! I will make your wish come true!!*

Alright it is time!! We need to get back to Bitcoin... let's talk about upgrades.

Chapter-23

Lightning Network

Bitcoin, while revolutionary as a decentralized digital currency, faces scalability issues that can limit its ability to handle a large volume of transactions. As the Bitcoin network grew in popularity, transaction fees and confirmation times began to rise, leading to concerns about Bitcoin's ability to scale for everyday use. We need a solution and we need it yesterday, enter the Lightning Network: a Layer 2 solution designed to resolve these scalability challenges while preserving Bitcoin's decentralized nature.

What is the Lightning Network?

The Lightning Network (LN) is a second-layer protocol built on top of Bitcoin that enables fast, low-cost transactions by moving most transactions off-chain, while still maintaining the security and decentralization of the main Bitcoin blockchain.

It does this by allowing users to create payment channels between one another, where multiple transactions can be made without broadcasting every single one to the Bitcoin network. Instead, only the opening and closing of the channel are recorded on the blockchain.

The concept of the Lightning Network was first proposed in 2015 by Joseph Poon and Thaddeus Dryja, who recognized that Bitcoin's scalability issues could be mitigated by enabling off-chain transactions, thus reducing the load on the main chain.

How Does the Lightning Network Work?

The Lightning Network functions by creating payment channels between two parties. These channels allow for multiple transactions to take place without involving the Bitcoin blockchain until the channel is closed. Here's a breakdown of the process:

To open a Lightning Network channel, two users (Shin and Satoshi) commit a certain amount of Bitcoin to a multisignature address. This commitment is recorded on the Bitcoin blockchain. Once the channel is open, they can conduct transactions with each other off-chain.

As long as the channel remains open, Shin and Satoshi can exchange Bitcoin back and forth. These transactions are not recorded on the Bitcoin blockchain, meaning they are fast and cheap. Each transaction updates the balances in the channel, but these changes are only reflected locally in the channel and not on the main blockchain.

Each time a transaction is made between Shin and Satoshi, both parties sign a new transaction with the updated state. This process ensures that the most recent transaction is valid and prevents fraud or double-spending.

When both are done transacting or want to settle the final balance, they can close the channel. The last agreed-upon state (which reflects all the off-chain transactions) is broadcast to the Bitcoin blockchain, and the final balances are settled. This closure transaction is recorded on the blockchain, and the Bitcoin is distributed according to the final balance of the payment channel.

The fascinating and one of the most powerful features of the Lightning Network is its ability to route payments across multiple channels. If A wants to pay C, but they don't have a direct channel, the Lightning Network can find a route through intermediaries B and D, allowing the payment to flow from A to C. This is known as the "network effect," where a large number of interconnected channels can create a global payment network.

The Benefits of the Lightning Network

The Lightning Network's most significant advantage is scalability. Since most transactions occur off-chain, the burden on the Bitcoin blockchain is reduced. This means that Bitcoin can process millions of transactions per second, compared to the main Bitcoin blockchain's 7 transactions per second. The off-chain nature of Lightning Network transactions allows for a vast number of microtransactions, making Bitcoin a feasible solution for everyday purchases, such as buying coffee or paying for digital services.

Lightning Network mitigates one of the major criticisms of Bitcoin in its early years, the high cost of transactions, especially during times of network congestion. With the help of Lightning Network, transactions are almost fee-less, as they are conducted off-chain. The fees that do exist are negligible compared to the fees on the Bitcoin mainchain. This makes Bitcoin more attractive for small payments, which was a primary challenge for its use as a practical currency.

And unlike Bitcoin transactions, which require confirmation by miners (taking an average of 10 minutes), Lightning Network transactions are instant. This is a crucial benefit for real-time payments, such as point-of-sale purchases or gaming microtransactions. By eliminating the need to wait for block confirmations, users can send and receive Bitcoin payments instantly.

The Lightning Network also enables microtransactions, where users can send very small amounts of Bitcoin that wouldn't be cost-effective to send directly on the main Bitcoin network. For instance, users could make a one-cent purchase or pay for a fraction of a service. Additionally, the Lightning Network supports more complex use cases, such as smart contracts and streaming payments, making it a versatile tool for developers and businesses and it prevents UTXO fragmentation too.

The Lightning Network's introduction has profound implications for Bitcoin's future as well. It allows Bitcoin to scale beyond its current limits and position itself as a true global payment network. The ability to process millions of transactions per second without congestion or high fees makes Bitcoin a competitor to traditional payment systems like Visa or PayPal.

Additionally, the Lightning Network makes Bitcoin more accessible to everyday users. By providing fast, inexpensive transactions, it enables Bitcoin to be used for real-world purchases, rather than just as a store of value. This is crucial for Bitcoin's adoption as a practical currency.

Moreover, the Lightning Network helps Bitcoin maintain its decentralized nature. Traditional scaling solutions, such as increasing the block size limit, could potentially lead to centralization, where only well-funded miners or full nodes could afford to process large blocks. By moving transactions off-chain, the Lightning Network reduces the strain on the main chain, preserving Bitcoin's decentralized ethos.

Challenges and Criticisms of the Lightning Network

The Lightning Network relies on users locking up funds in payment channels, which could lead to liquidity issues. If a channel is not funded properly, transactions could fail or be delayed. Additionally, routing payments across multiple channels requires each participant to have enough liquidity to facilitate the transaction, which can be a challenge for smaller or less popular nodes.

As the Lightning Network grows, the complexity of routing payments across many channels also increases. For large or complex payments, finding a route with sufficient liquidity can become difficult, which may result in failed payments or delays. Solutions to this problem are still being developed, such as more sophisticated routing algorithms and the creation of liquidity management tools.

Although the Lightning Network is designed to maintain decentralization, there are concerns that large payment channels could lead to centralization. If a few entities control the majority of liquidity in the network, they could potentially exert influence over the network's routing and transaction processing. However, the open-source and permissionless nature of Bitcoin ensures that anyone can participate in the Lightning Network, and efforts are being made to prevent centralization.

Even though Lightning Network has grown rapidly since its inception, widespread adoption is still in its early stages. For the network to reach its full potential, more businesses and users must adopt it. As of now, only a small percentage of Bitcoin users and merchants actively use the Lightning Network, but this is expected to grow as technology and infrastructure continue to develop.

Having said all that, the Lightning Network is one of the most promising solutions to Bitcoin's scalability issues, enabling fast, low-cost, and scalable transactions. By allowing off-chain payments, the Lightning Network enhances Bitcoin's ability to handle millions of transactions per second and supports microtransactions, making Bitcoin more practical for everyday use. While the network faces challenges in terms of liquidity, routing, and adoption, its potential to revolutionize Bitcoin as a global payment system is undeniable.

As Bitcoin continues to evolve, the Lightning Network will play a critical role in making Bitcoin not just a store of value but a fully functional, global currency.

Chapter -24

Segregated Witness (SegWit): Scaling Bitcoin for the Future

In the history of Bitcoin's development, one of the most crucial upgrades was the implementation of Segregated Witness, commonly known as SegWit. Activated in 2017, SegWit addressed several key challenges facing Bitcoin, particularly the block size war.

In this chapter, we will explore what SegWit is, how it works, and the impact it has had on the Bitcoin network. But before that we need to talk about the block size war.

Once started as a mere thought, increasing the bitcoin block size from 1Mb to a required size turned into an all-right war from 2015-2017.

There were two sides, big blockers and small blockers. Big blockers wanted an increase in block size and the small blockers wanted to stick with the 1MB block size which was set by Satoshi in 2010.

Increasing the block size can accommodate more transactions in a block but it had to be done through a Hard Fork (an irreversible, and non-backwards compatible code split). This will disregard the old chain and the new hard forked chain will be used.

An increase in size means an increase in data too. That means small miners cannot handle huge data in the future as the network grows. Started as a debate ended in death threats to developers and in the end the small blockers won. As bitcoin doesn't have a CEO the miners had to cast a vote to accept the change or deny it. In the end miners voted for the existing block size.

It was not a pleasant time; the community was divided and all sorts of stuff were happening. Let us just not take sides here and honestly, I don't want to take sides either. What happened, happened. What we gonna do look into is, from this war we came up with a solution called SegWit.

What is Segregated Witness?

Segregated Witness is a protocol upgrade that fundamentally changes how Bitcoin transactions are stored in blocks. It separates (or "segregates") the witness data—the digital signatures that validate a transaction—from the transaction data itself. This separation allows for more efficient use of block space, thus increasing Bitcoin's transaction throughput without needing to increase the block size limit.

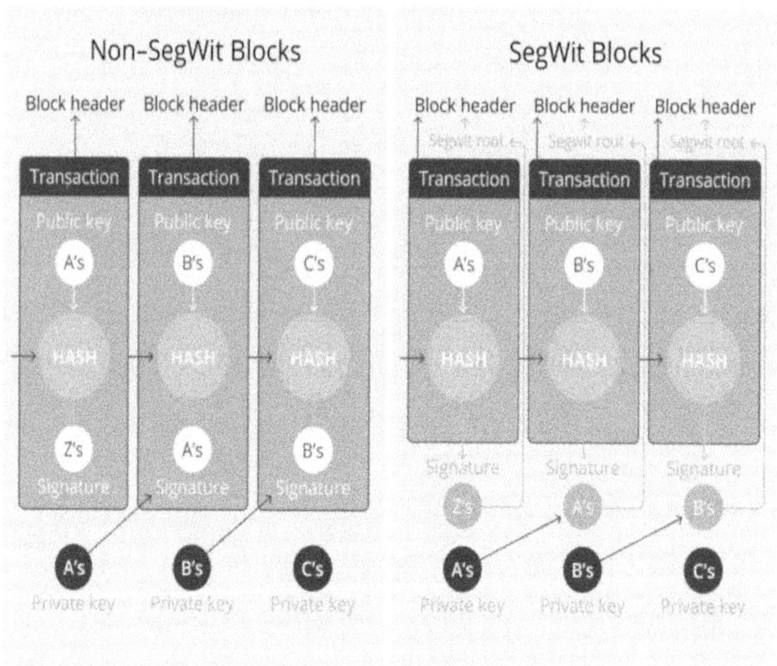

SegWit vs non-SegWit block..

The term "Segregated Witness" comes from the fact that the witness data, which contains cryptographic signatures verifying the legitimacy of a transaction, is moved to a different section of the block, separate from the main transaction data. By doing this, Bitcoin blocks can accommodate more transactions per block.

As we discussed one of Bitcoin's major bottlenecks before SegWit was its block size limit. Bitcoin's blocks were capped at 1 MB, and each block could contain only a limited number of transactions. As Bitcoin's popularity grew, the network faced increasing congestion, leading to higher transaction fees and slower processing times.

At peak demand, users who wanted to send transactions would often have to pay higher fees to ensure their transactions were included in the next block. Additionally, the block size limit led to a situation where the network was not able to handle a large volume of transactions, thus hindering Bitcoin's ability to scale effectively.

The limitation of 1 MB per block is not arbitrary. It was put in place by Bitcoin's creator, Satoshi Nakamoto, to ensure that the network remained decentralized by limiting the block size. Larger blocks would require more computational power and disk space, potentially leading to centralization as only well-funded entities could afford to store and process large amounts of blockchain data. Also, if bitcoin does not have a block size, anyone can create a large enough block which can put a great deal of stress on Nodes compromising security of the network.

However, as Bitcoin gained popularity, this cap became a significant impediment to scalability.

SegWit: The Technical Details

The original structure of a Bitcoin transaction looks like this:

Transaction Inputs: Specifies which previous transactions are being spent.

Transaction Outputs: Details where the bitcoins are being sent (i.e., the recipient's address).

Transaction Signatures (Witness Data): Cryptographic signatures that confirm the transaction is valid and authorized by the private key holder.

SegWit changes this structure by moving the witness data (signatures) outside the main transaction body. This new structure does not change the overall logic of Bitcoin transactions but optimizes how the data is stored. By segregating the witness data, it reduces the size of the transaction that needs to be stored on the blockchain.

In essence, the SegWit upgrade redefines the way block size is calculated. While the 1 MB limit remains for the transaction data, SegWit transactions are more space-efficient because the witness data is stored separately. This enables the network to process more transactions within the same block size, enhancing scalability.

The technical aspect of SegWit is accomplished through a soft fork, meaning that nodes that do not implement SegWit can still participate in the network without any disruption. However, to fully utilize SegWit's benefits, users and services must adopt SegWit-compatible addresses.

One of the most immediate benefits of SegWit is the increased transaction throughput per block. On average, SegWit transactions are about 40-60% more space-efficient compared to legacy transactions, (Yeah! A signature takes that amount of space in a Tx) allowing more transactions to be processed with the same block size. This means more users can transact on the Bitcoin network without causing congestion or higher fees.

A SegWit block has 3MB for signature data and the pre-existing 1MB of block size. So, unlike the popular opinion, SegWit is an increase to block size.

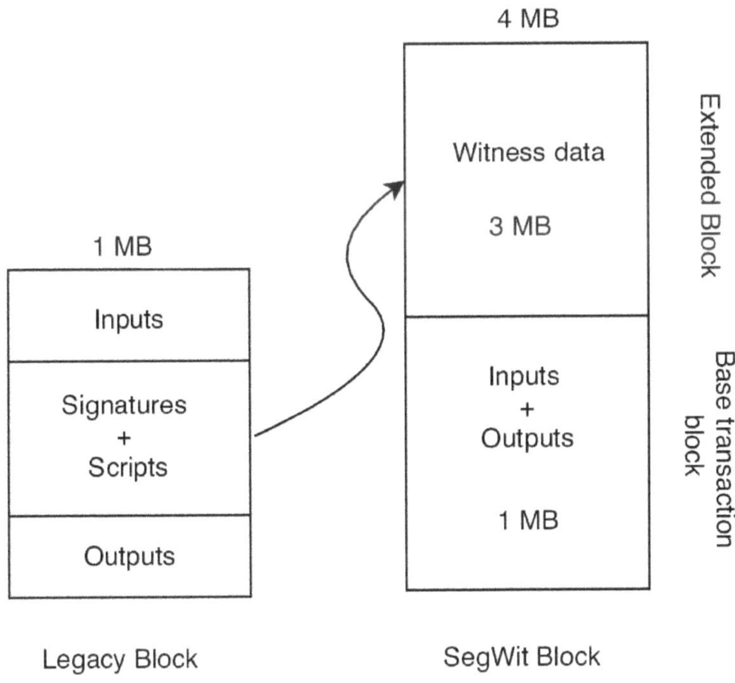

Before SegWit, one of Bitcoin's vulnerabilities was its susceptibility to transaction malleability. This meant that the transaction ID (TXID) could be altered by changing the signature data. For example, Satoshi sent me some bitcoin and is waiting for confirmation, before confirmation I buy a car from you using the same bitcoin which is also unconfirmed and I leave the showroom.

As I got out of the showroom Satoshi altered the signature slightly and changes the TXID. TXID is created by hashing the transaction data. Let say he altered a value from 1 to 01 in the Tx data and rest all are unchanged. The mathematical value is the same but we know that SHA256 will give a different output even if there is a slight modification. This results in a change in the TXID. Even though the ID is changed I will receive the bitcoin due to the vulnerability in bitcoin (Tx with altered TXID will get confirmed) but unfortunately you won't receive the payment I sent as it will be marked as invalid because your bitcoin came from the first Tx Satoshi sent me which does not exist anymore. Lucky me!!!

 Such malleability created issues for certain applications, especially for second-layer solutions like the Lightning Network, which rely on immutable transaction IDs.

SegWit fixes this issue by separating the witness data from the rest of the transaction. With the signatures no longer being part of the transaction's hash, the TXID becomes immutable. This allows for more secure and predictable interactions between applications and the Bitcoin network.

SegWit indirectly reduces transaction fees as well by improving the efficiency of the Bitcoin network. Because more transactions can fit in a block, there is less competition for block space, and thus, users are less likely to be forced to pay high fees to get their transactions included in a timely manner. This leads to a more predictable fee market.

In addition, SegWit transactions are more efficient in terms of byte size. Users who adopt SegWit addresses (starting with "3") can benefit from lower fees due to the reduced size of their transactions. As the network becomes more optimized, fee volatility is reduced, making Bitcoin a more reliable payment system.

When SegWit was introduced, Tx was measured by weight instead of the previous measurement by size approach. And of course we have a formula for that.

Base Tx size (no witness data) * 3 + Full Tx size

Legacy bitcoin Tx cannot strip the witness data so they always equal 4 times the Tx size.

For example, a 1000 Bytes Legacy Tx will have a size of

1000*3+1000 = 4000

A SegWit Tx of 1200 Bytes with 800 Bytes of Base Tx and 400 Bytes Witness Data will have a size of

(1200-400) * 3+1200=3600

Although in theory SegWit has an extended block of 4MB but in practice it usual creates a block of 2MB.

SegWit and Lightning Network go hand in hand.

The Lightning Network relies on SegWit to securely create multi-signature transactions, and by fixing the transaction malleability problem, SegWit makes it feasible to create these off-chain payment channels. Without SegWit, the Lightning Network's functionality would have been compromised.

SegWit thus acts as a catalyst for Bitcoin's long-term scalability by enabling Layer 2 solutions to operate effectively.

Because of all the issues regarding the block size It wasn't a warm welcome for SegWit

While SegWit was activated in 2017, its adoption has been gradual. Initially, many Bitcoin users and services were hesitant to upgrade to SegWit-compatible addresses due to concerns about compatibility and the perceived complexity of the transition. However, over time, more and more wallets, exchanges, and services have adopted SegWit as it became clear that the benefits outweighed the costs.

One of the challenges SegWit faces is the fact that Bitcoin's block size limit still exists, and there is a trade-off between adopting SegWit and increasing the block size limit. Bitcoin community pushed for larger blocks through a hard fork. However, SegWit's soft-fork approach has ultimately allowed for a more gradual and less disruptive scaling process.

Let us forget the past and admit the fact that it is necessary to make bitcoin future proof, some wanted a size increase and some didn't, we agreed on an upgrade and Segregated Witness represents a monumental step forward for Bitcoin's scalability and security. By optimizing the way transactions are stored on the blockchain, SegWit helped Bitcoin to handle more transactions, lower fees, and fix issues like transaction malleability. The benefits of SegWit are clear, and its implementation has paved the way for further scaling solutions, such as the Lightning Network.

It doesn't end here, there always more to Bitcoin. Enter "Native SegWit"

Chapter 25

Native SegWit: A Revolutionary Upgrade to Bitcoin's Transaction Model

One of the most significant upgrades to Bitcoin's protocol was the introduction of Segregated Witness (SegWit) in 2017.

However, SegWit itself came in two forms: P2SH-SegWit (Pay-to-Script-Hash SegWit) and Native SegWit (also known as Bech32 SegWit). While both forms of SegWit aim to improve Bitcoin's scalability and efficiency, Native SegWit introduced a new, more efficient way of handling Bitcoin transactions that has become the preferred option for many users and services.

Native SegWit (also known as Bech32 SegWit) refers to a specific implementation of SegWit that uses a new address format, Bech32, for Bitcoin transactions. While P2SH-SegWit addresses are compatible with older Bitcoin wallets and addresses, Native SegWit addresses are a more modern solution that takes full advantage of SegWit's benefits, offering higher efficiency and better support for scalability.

First bitcoin addresses used Legacy address or P2PKH address which had larger transaction size and resulted in high fees and slower speeds. SegWit introduced Pay-to-script-

Hash or P2SH which enabled users to spend BTC based on the satisfaction of the script's hash that has been specified in a transaction.

Native SegWit transactions are those that use the Bech32 format for their addresses, which begins with the prefix **bc1.** These addresses are distinct from traditional Bitcoin addresses (which begin with 1 for P2PKH addresses and 3 for P2SH addresses) and are considered to be more efficient and error-resistant.

The fundamental change that Native SegWit introduces is the format and structure of Bitcoin addresses. Here's a breakdown of how Native SegWit works:

Native SegWit uses the Bech32 address format, which is designed to be more efficient and user-friendly than previous formats. Bech32 addresses start with bc1 and are followed by a string of alphanumeric characters that represent a SegWit address.

Native SegWit transactions like SegWit separate the witness data (signatures) from the rest of the transaction. By placing the witness data outside of the transaction body.
However, unlike **P2SH-SegWit** addresses, which are a SegWit transaction wrapped in a Pay-to-Script-Hash (P2SH) address, Native SegWit eliminates the need for a P2SH

wrapper, making it more efficient. The absence of the P2SH layer means that the addresses are simpler and the transactions are smaller in size.

Instead of a wrapper Native SegWit locks fund to the hash of a witness program directly. When the owner spends the funds, they are required to provide only the witness program and the witness that satisfies it.

Native SegWit transactions also use a new script version, which allows Bitcoin to handle newer and more complex types of scripts in the future. This helps ensure that Bitcoin's transaction model can continue to evolve without compatibility issues.

Benefits of Native SegWit

Native SegWit addresses provide several key benefits over traditional Bitcoin addresses and even over P2SH-SegWit. These include:

Because Native SegWit transactions are smaller in size (due to the separation of witness data), they require less space in a block. This allows more transactions to fit within a block, which leads to **lower transaction fees** for users.

With smaller transaction sizes and more efficient use of block space, Native SegWit transactions can be processed more quickly, reducing the time it takes for transactions to be confirmed.

By reducing the size of each transaction, Native SegWit increases the number of transactions that can be processed per block. This is a crucial improvement for Bitcoin's scalability, enabling it to handle more users and more transactions without running into congestion issues.

The Bech32 address format used by Native SegWit is more robust and resistant to errors compared to traditional address formats. It uses a checksum to ensure the validity of addresses, reducing the likelihood of mistakes when entering or sharing Bitcoin addresses.

Native SegWit's flexibility with script versioning makes it a more adaptable solution for future upgrades to the Bitcoin network. It paves the way for future innovations, such as smart contracts and more advanced features, without breaking compatibility with existing systems.

Native SegWit vs P2SH-SegWit

While both Native SegWit and P2SH-SegWit provide the benefits of SegWit—such as reducing transaction size and improving scalability—the two differ in key areas:

Address Format: P2SH-SegWit addresses begin with 3, while Native SegWit addresses start with bc1. The Bech32 format used by Native SegWit is more efficient and user-friendly.

Efficiency: Native SegWit transactions are more efficient than P2SH-SegWit because they do not need the additional P2SH wrapper. This results in smaller transaction sizes and therefore lower fees and faster processing.

Compatibility: P2SH-SegWit is compatible with legacy Bitcoin addresses, meaning users can send Bitcoin to P2SH-SegWit addresses from older wallets. However, Native SegWit requires support from wallets and services that are updated to handle Bech32 addresses. Although support for Native SegWit is growing, it is still less widespread than P2SH-SegWit.

Native SegWit adoption has been growing, but many Bitcoin wallets and exchanges still prioritize P2SH-SegWit for compatibility reasons. However, as Native SegWit offers better scalability and efficiency, its adoption is expected to continue increasing.

Challenges and Adoption of Native SegWit

While Native SegWit offers clear advantages, its adoption has been slower than anticipated for several reasons:

Many exchanges and wallets are still in the process of implementing full support for Bech32 addresses. Until there is broader adoption, users may be reluctant to fully embrace Native SegWit.

The Bech32 address format is unfamiliar to many users, especially those who have used traditional Bitcoin addresses that start with 1 or 3. However, as more wallets and services integrate Native SegWit, the learning curve is expected to reduce.

Transitioning from the legacy system to Native SegWit requires a shift in how Bitcoin transactions are structured and processed. While this is an essential step for Bitcoin's long-term scalability, it may take time for all parts of the ecosystem to adopt the upgrade fully.

Despite these challenges, the benefits of Native SegWit, especially in terms of scalability and transaction efficiency, are undeniable. As support continues to grow, Native SegWit will play an increasingly important role in the future of Bitcoin.

To use Native SegWit, users need a wallet that supports Bech32 addresses. Many popular wallets, including Electrum, Blue Wallet, and Bitcoin Core, now support Native SegWit by default. When sending Bitcoin, the wallet will automatically generate a Bech32 address, and users can benefit from reduced fees and faster processing times.

As Bitcoin continues to evolve, the widespread adoption of Native SegWit is crucial for the network's long-term scalability. While adoption may take time, the future of Bitcoin's transaction model will increasingly rely on the efficiencies introduced by Native SegWit, ensuring that Bitcoin remains a fast, secure, and low-cost method of transferring value globally.

Chapter-26

Taproot: Enhancing Bitcoin's Smart Contract capabilities and Privacy.

Bitcoin's original design was focused on providing a secure and decentralized currency. However, as the ecosystem grew, so did the demand for more advanced functionality, such as smart contracts, privacy features, and scalability solutions. Taproot, introduced in November 2021, is one of Bitcoin's most important protocol upgrades since SegWit. It enhances Bitcoin's privacy, flexibility, and scalability while making smart contracts more accessible and efficient.

What is Taproot?

Taproot is a soft fork to the Bitcoin protocol that introduces several important features aimed at improving the privacy and scalability of Bitcoin transactions. The upgrade primarily focuses on optimizing smart contracts, privacy, and transaction efficiency. Taproot was activated in November 2021, following a lengthy process of research, development, and community discussion.

Taproot builds on previous Bitcoin upgrades, such as SegWit, and introduces new cryptographic techniques to enhance

Bitcoin's functionality without compromising its security or decentralization.

At its core, Taproot integrates **Schnorr signatures** with a new way of structuring smart contracts, allowing Bitcoin to become more flexible and private. The main components of Taproot are:

Schnorr Signatures: Taproot replaces Bitcoin's original ECDSA (Elliptic Curve Digital Signature Algorithm) with Schnorr signatures. This is a significant improvement because Schnorr signatures are simpler, more efficient, and support batch verification. They also allow for the creation of multi-signature transactions that look the same as single-signature transactions, improving privacy.

Mast (Merkelized Abstract Syntax Trees): Taproot introduces a new way to structure complex smart contracts using Merkelized Abstract Syntax Trees (MAST). MAST enables Bitcoin transactions to encode multiple conditions (e.g., smart contracts) in a way that only the executed conditions are revealed, improving both privacy and scalability. With MAST, if a multi-signature or conditional transaction is executed, only the specific contract used is revealed, minimizing the exposure of other potential conditions that could have been used in the transaction.

Tapscript:

Taproot also introduces Tapscript, a new scripting language that enables more complex and efficient smart contracts on Bitcoin. It is a refined version of Bitcoin's existing scripting language, Script, designed to work seamlessly with Taproot. Tapscript enables more flexible, modular, and private smart contracts while maintaining compatibility with existing Bitcoin scripts.

Taproot Outputs:

Taproot allows users to create outputs that can be spent in different ways, such as through a simple public key or a more complex script. This feature helps to unify Bitcoin's transaction model, making it easier to create complex smart contracts without increasing transaction size or compromising privacy.

Taproot brings several important benefits to Bitcoin, particularly around privacy, scalability, and smart contract capabilities. Let's explore these in more detail:

Taproot improves Bitcoin's privacy by making complex transactions (such as multi-signature or conditional smart contracts) indistinguishable from regular Bitcoin transactions. Before Taproot, transactions with multi-signatures or scripts were easily distinguishable on the blockchain, revealing more information than necessary. With Taproot, only the executed script (or public key) is revealed, preventing the leakage of potentially sensitive information. This makes Bitcoin transactions more private, even for users engaging in complex smart contracts.

By reducing the size of transactions that involve complex scripts or multi-signature setups, Taproot helps increase Bitcoin's scalability. Since fewer data points need to be recorded on the blockchain, more transactions can fit into each block, increasing the overall throughput of the network. The improved efficiency of Taproot's transaction structure helps to keep transaction fees lower, making Bitcoin more cost-effective for users.

With Taproot, users can create more efficient multi-signature transactions that do not require the same amount of data as before. This reduces the size of the transaction, resulting in lower fees. Additionally, Taproot makes it possible to execute more complex contracts in a more space-efficient manner, which also reduces the overall cost of using Bitcoin for these contracts.

Taproot enables more complex and flexible smart contracts by introducing the MAST protocol and Tapscript. MAST allows Bitcoin to encode multiple conditions for spending coins, but only the relevant one is revealed when the transaction is executed. This enhances both privacy and scalability by reducing the data needed for smart contracts and making it more efficient to implement them on the blockchain.

As we said earlier, Taproot is a soft fork, meaning it is backward-compatible with previous versions of the Bitcoin protocol. This ensures that Bitcoin's existing ecosystem, including wallets, exchanges, and other services, can continue to function without disruption while still benefiting from the enhancements Taproot brings. The upgrade does not force any immediate changes to how Bitcoin transactions work, making it easier for the community to adopt.

When we talk about Taproot the one thing, I get most excited about is Schnorr Signatures.

Schnorr Signatures: The Backbone of Taproot

Schnorr signatures are a significant cryptographic improvement over the ECDSA signatures used previously in Bitcoin. Satoshi did not use Schnorr in the first place mainly due to two reasons, in cryptography and cryptographers in general only accept systems which are time tested and Schnorr Signatures were relatively new at the time when compared to ECDSA. And secondly if my knowledge is correct (I shouldn't have said that) Schnorr Signatures were patented and we had to wait till now for it to expire.

Schnorr signatures allow for **batch signing**, meaning multiple transactions can be signed in a single operation, reducing the computational load and improving efficiency.

One of the most notable features of Schnorr signatures is the ability to **aggregate** multiple signatures into a single signature. This means that a multi-signature transaction, which previously required multiple signatures to be recorded, can now appear as a single signature. This reduces the size of multi-signature transactions and improves privacy by making them look like regular transactions.

Schnorr signatures also allow for **non-interactive** multi-signatures, meaning that all participants in a multi-signature scheme can sign the transaction independently, without needing to communicate with each other. This improves usability and reduces the potential for errors.

Schnorr signatures offer better security properties compared to ECDSA. They are resistant to certain types of attacks, such as signature malleability, and offer a more flexible structure for creating smart contracts. Before Taproot, Bitcoin had limited functionality for smart contracts, which allowed for conditional transactions and other advanced use cases but in a relatively basic way. Taproot significantly enhances Bitcoin's ability to handle complex smart contracts.

Taproot allows for more complex smart contracts and conditional transactions to be written in Bitcoin's scripting language. This includes multi-signature setups, payment channels, and various other types of conditional contracts, all of which can now be implemented more efficiently.

The main point is, Taproot reduces the cost of creating these contracts as well by enabling them to be executed with lower overhead. Moreover, the privacy improvements ensure that only the executed script is revealed, protecting the parties involved in the contract from unnecessary exposure.

With Taproot's ability to handle more complex smart contracts, it opens the door for more DeFi (Decentralized Finance) applications and Layer-2 solutions on Bitcoin. Taproot makes it easier to implement features like atomic swaps, decentralized exchanges, and more, which were previously difficult or costly to execute on Bitcoin's original script.

Bitcoin, DeFi, smart contracts, privacy, atomic swaps, never in my wildest dreams I thought I will be mentioning everything in one sentence! Gosh we are lucky to be alive in this era!

Since Taproot was activated, its adoption has been steadily growing. Major Bitcoin wallets, such as Electrum and Bitcoin Core, now support Taproot, and many services are beginning to take advantage of its privacy and scalability improvements. However, widespread adoption of Taproot in all parts of the Bitcoin ecosystem will take time.

As more tools and infrastructure are developed to support Taproot's full capabilities, we can expect to see new and innovative use cases for Bitcoin, especially in areas such as smart contracts, privacy, and decentralized finance.

While Taproot is still in the early stages of adoption, its potential to unlock Bitcoin's full capabilities makes it one of the most important developments in the history of Bitcoin. With time, Taproot will enable more powerful and private transactions, opening new possibilities for Bitcoin as a platform for decentralized applications and smart contracts.

Chapter-27

OP_CAT: A Proposed Bitcoin Upgrade for Enhanced Functionality

Bitcoin's scripting language, Script, has long been a foundational element of its programmability, enabling basic conditional transactions and locking mechanisms. However, the capabilities of Bitcoin's Script language have been somewhat limited in comparison to more flexible blockchain platforms like Ethereum because as we know the Bitcoin script is not turing complete. To overcome some of these limitations, the Bitcoin community has explored the idea of adding new operations to Script, one of which is **OP_CAT**.

OP_CAT (short for "Concatenate") is an operation that was once part of Bitcoin's Script language but was disabled in the early years of the network due to security concerns. Recently, there has been increasing interest in the potential reactivation and use of OP_CAT, especially with the ongoing development of Bitcoin's smart contract capabilities.

OP_CAT is an operation in Bitcoin's Script language designed to concatenate two pieces of data. In simple terms, it would take two items on the stack and combine them into one, allowing for more sophisticated data manipulations. The result of the concatenation operation would be placed back onto the stack, allowing further operations to take place.

For example, if you had two items:

- A = "Hello"
- B = "World"

The execution of OP_CAT would result in:

- A + B = "HelloWorld"

No Stack pictures this time, you guys are matured enough to visualize now.

While this might seem like a minor operation, its potential implications for Bitcoin's programmability are far-reaching. By reintroducing OP_CAT, Bitcoin could support more advanced scripting capabilities, opening the door to new use cases, including smart contracts, complex signatures, and transaction flexibility.

As I briefly mentioned, OP_CAT was originally part of the Bitcoin Script language, but it was disabled due to concerns about its security. Specifically, the operation was found to have certain vulnerabilities that could potentially be exploited in a way that could lead to stack overflow or denial-of-service (DoS) attacks. These attacks could cause Bitcoin nodes to crash or behave unexpectedly if the OP_CAT operation was executed in a maliciously constructed transaction. Remember nonstandard scripts and nodes declining it?

The specific problem stemmed from the fact that OP_CAT required a significant number of computational resources to process large pieces of data. If an attacker were able to craft transactions that repeatedly concatenated enormous data chunks, it could overwhelm a node, leading to crashes or delays. In Bitcoin's early years, the network's primary focus was on simplicity, security, and stability. As a result, OP_CAT was disabled to mitigate these risks.

Despite the security concerns, the idea of re-enabling OP_CAT has been revisited over the years. As Bitcoin's ecosystem has matured and security measures have been strengthened, there is growing interest in enabling more advanced functionality within Bitcoin's Script. Reactivating OP_CAT could provide several benefits for Bitcoin's capabilities, as it would enable a wider range of script-based applications.

The reactivation of OP_CAT would require careful consideration of potential security vulnerabilities, and a number of safeguards would need to be introduced. For example, Bitcoin developers would need to establish limits on the size and complexity of data that can be concatenated, as well as mechanisms to prevent resource exhaustion or DoS attacks. Any such reactivation would also involve rigorous testing, community consensus, and a soft fork to ensure backward compatibility.

If OP_CAT were re-enabled, there are a variety of scenarios in which it could be used to enhance Bitcoin's functionality. Some potential use cases include:

Smart Contracts and Conditional Payments: OP_CAT could be used in the development of more complex smart contracts. For instance, it could allow for more flexible conditional scripts, where multiple pieces of data need to be combined to trigger a valid transaction. This could enable the creation of more sophisticated contract logic without the need for more complex blockchain platforms like Ethereum.

Enhanced Multi-Signature Transactions: Multi-signature schemes could benefit from OP_CAT by allowing for the combination of various public keys or signatures into a single, compact data structure. This could lead to more efficient multi-sig setups where multiple parties are required to sign off on a transaction, reducing the data footprint and simplifying the contract logic.

Transaction Compression: OP_CAT could help in compressing or combining transaction data. By allowing different parts of a transaction (e.g., signatures, public keys, or other metadata) to be concatenated, Bitcoin transactions could become more space-efficient, lowering the cost and improving scalability.

Bitcoin Privacy Enhancements: Combining multiple pieces of data with OP_CAT could also provide privacy improvements. By concatenating various data elements in a way that obscures their individual meanings, OP_CAT could be used to make transactions more anonymous or harder to trace.

Chainlink and Oracles: OP_CAT could enhance Bitcoin's ability to interact with **oracles** and other off-chain data sources. By concatenating on-chain and off-chain data, it would be possible to build more intricate **decentralized finance (DeFi)** applications that interact with the real world, including price feeds, weather data, or other external inputs.

Think about the amount of growth Bitcoin will get if we could build an ecosystem like Ethereum. It is easier said than done, yeah, I agree, but we have to face the music and need to find solutions to make bitcoin future proof. Whenever I hear about a Bitcoin upgrade immediately, I get PTSD about the block size war that happened. The reactivation of OP_CAT would not be without its challenges. Some of the primary concerns and areas of focus include:

Security Risks: As mentioned earlier, OP_CAT was originally disabled due to security risks such as stack overflow and DoS attacks. To mitigate these risks, Bitcoin developers would need to implement robust rate **limiting** and **data size restrictions** to prevent malicious actors from exploiting the operation.

Code Complexity: Enabling OP_CAT would increase the complexity of Bitcoin's scripting language. More complex scripts can be harder to audit and may inadvertently introduce new bugs or vulnerabilities, which could affect the network's stability and security.

Backward Compatibility: Any changes to Bitcoin's Script language must maintain backward compatibility to ensure that the network does not break existing wallets, exchanges, or services. A soft fork could allow for the reactivation of OP_CAT without disrupting the overall Bitcoin protocol.

Community Consensus: The decision to reactivate OP_CAT would require broad consensus from the Bitcoin community, including developers, miners, and node operators. Given that Bitcoin's upgrade process is highly decentralized and requires widespread agreement, the reactivation of OP_CAT would need significant support to move forward.

While the reactivation of OP_CAT is still a topic of discussion, it represents the growing interest in expanding Bitcoin's programmability. As Bitcoin continues to evolve, there may be other opportunities for enhancing its scripting language and adding new features that improve its functionality.

However, Bitcoin's development process is slow and deliberate, prioritizing security and stability above all else. The addition of OP_CAT could lead to exciting new use cases for Bitcoin, but any changes must be thoroughly tested and carefully considered to maintain the integrity of the network.

OP_CAT represents a fascinating potential upgrade to Bitcoin's Script language, offering a way to enhance Bitcoin's capabilities and open the door to more complex smart contracts, privacy features, and transaction types. While OP_CAT was disabled in the early days of Bitcoin due to security concerns, the idea of re-enabling it has resurfaced as part of Bitcoin's continued evolution. That is kind of macho as well, right? Its like I was afraid of something till yesterday and now I am like, bring it on!!!

The reactivation of OP_CAT sure as hell would require addressing security risks, maintaining backward compatibility, and ensuring broad consensus from the Bitcoin community. If successfully reintroduced, OP_CAT could significantly expand Bitcoin's programmability, enabling new use cases that extend its functionality while still maintaining the security and decentralization principles that Bitcoin is built upon.

As Bitcoin continues to mature, it is likely that future updates to the protocol will continue to explore ways to enhance its scripting capabilities. The potential reintroduction of OP_CAT is just one example of how Bitcoin could evolve to meet the needs of a more complex and dynamic cryptocurrency ecosystem.

Chapter-28

Ordinals on Bitcoin: Revolutionizing the Digital Asset Space

Bitcoin, the world's first decentralized cryptocurrency, has long been known for its simple design and use case as a store of value and a medium of exchange. Yeah!! Not anymore, recent developments have opened new possibilities for the Bitcoin blockchain, allowing it to support additional features beyond basic transactions. One of the most notable innovations is the **Ordinals protocol**, which enables Bitcoin to host unique, non-fungible tokens (NFTs) and other types of digital assets, creating new ways to use and interact with Bitcoin.

That's what I love about Bitcoin and its developers, first few chapters we were considering Bitcoin as a store of value, its fixed supply and all of that, suddenly now we are like showering with upgrades after upgrades. Honestly, from the bottom of my heart I enjoyed every bit of writing this book mate!

Note: The above paragraph was written when I was proof reading before publishing. I had to write that; I am sorry and I don't regret it by the way.

Coming back to the topic, introduced in 2023 by developer Casey Rodarmor, **Ordinals** take advantage of the existing Bitcoin block structure, allowing the embedding of arbitrary data into individual satoshis—the smallest unit of Bitcoin. This chapter explores the Ordinals protocol, how it works, its implications for Bitcoin's ecosystem, and how it's reshaping the future of the Bitcoin network.

Ordinals are a system for numbering and tracking individual **satoshis** on the Bitcoin blockchain. A satoshi is the smallest unit of Bitcoin, equivalent to one hundred millionth of a Bitcoin (0.00000001 BTC). While Bitcoin transactions typically focus on transferring Bitcoin from one address to another, Ordinals allow users to assign specific, traceable identifiers to each satoshi. This system opens the door to digital collectibles and NFTs on Bitcoin, similar to what Ethereum enabled with its ERC-721 tokens.

The key innovation of Ordinals lies in the ability to inscribe arbitrary data onto individual satoshis. This data can include text, images, videos, or even executable code, effectively turning each satoshi into a unique, programmable digital asset. These "inscriptions" are stored directly on the Bitcoin blockchain and inherit Bitcoin's security, immutability, and decentralization, creating a robust environment for digital assets.

The mechanics behind Ordinals are built on Bitcoin's **taproot** upgrade, which expanded the capacity of Bitcoin scripts and provided enhanced flexibility for data storage. Ordinals utilize a process called **inscription**, where data is attached to a satoshi through a specific script within the Bitcoin transaction. Here's how it works:

Satoshis and Ordinal Numbers: Each satoshi on the Bitcoin network is assigned a unique identifier called an "ordinal number," which tracks its position in the Bitcoin blockchain. As new transactions are confirmed, each satoshi is sequentially numbered, with each one becoming part of the overall Bitcoin history.

Inscriptions: To create an Ordinal, data is "inscribed" onto a specific satoshi. Inscriptions are essentially digital artifacts, such as images, text, or files, that are stored directly on the Bitcoin blockchain, allowing them to be uniquely identified and transacted.

Taproot's Role: The **taproot upgrade**, which activated in November 2021, laid the foundation for the Ordinals protocol by enabling more efficient and flexible data storage. Taproot's scripting improvements allow for greater complexity in transaction structures, which is critical for inscribing data onto Bitcoin in a way that doesn't bloat the blockchain or compromise security.

Transaction and Metadata: The inscription of data onto a satoshi is done by attaching metadata (the inscribed data) to specific Bitcoin transactions. Once an inscription is made, the data becomes a permanent part of the Bitcoin blockchain, just like regular transaction data. These inscriptions can be tracked, transferred, and traded, effectively creating **NFTs** on the Bitcoin network.

Ordinals and Bitcoin NFTs

One of the most exciting applications of Ordinals is the creation of **Bitcoin-based NFTs**. NFTs are unique digital assets that are verifiably scarce and represent ownership of a specific item or piece of content. Ordinals enable the creation of NFTs directly on Bitcoin's blockchain, without the need for a secondary layer like Ethereum's ERC-721 tokens.

How Bitcoin NFTs Differ from Ethereum NFTs: Traditionally, NFTs on Ethereum are created using smart contracts on the Ethereum blockchain. These contracts define the unique characteristics of the NFT, such as ownership, metadata, and transferability. Ordinals, on the other hand, inscribe the NFT data directly onto individual satoshis, which are recorded on the Bitcoin blockchain itself. This means that the NFTs created through Ordinals do not rely on smart contracts or additional layers, but instead use Bitcoin's existing infrastructure.

Inscribing Digital Art: Artists and creators can inscribe their digital works onto Bitcoin through Ordinals, turning their creations into unique, provably scarce assets on the blockchain. This has opened up a new frontier for digital art, as artists can now leverage Bitcoin's established reputation for security and decentralization to mint NFTs.

Collectibles and Gaming: Just like other blockchains, Ordinals enable the creation of collectibles and assets for games. By using Bitcoin as the underlying infrastructure for these assets, Ordinals NFTs have the potential to become the foundation for Bitcoin-based digital economies, allowing for the creation and exchange of virtual goods on a decentralized network.

The introduction of Ordinals expands Bitcoin's utility beyond a store of value or medium of exchange, introducing a range of potential use cases:

Digital Collectibles: Just as NFTs on Ethereum have given rise to virtual art, collectibles, and digital ownership, Ordinals enable a similar use case on Bitcoin. Artists, creators, and collectors now have the ability to create and trade Bitcoin-native digital assets, giving Bitcoin a broader role in the world of digital content.

Tokenizing Physical Assets: Ordinals can also be used to tokenize real-world assets, such as real estate, collectibles, or luxury items. By attaching unique identifiers to satoshis, physical assets can be represented on the Bitcoin blockchain, providing a transparent and secure way to transfer ownership.

Immutable Recordkeeping: The ability to inscribe data onto Bitcoin could be used for a range of **decentralized applications** (dApps), such as verifiable certificates, immutable records, or digital identities. Inscriptions could represent everything from academic credentials to legal documents, ensuring data permanence and tamper-proof storage on the Bitcoin blockchain.

While Bitcoin is not as well known for its DeFi ecosystem as Ethereum, the Ordinals protocol offers the possibility of introducing DeFi-like functionality to Bitcoin. Through the use of inscriptions, Bitcoin could support decentralized lending, staking, and other financial instruments, creating new ways for users to interact with Bitcoin as a financial asset.

The Impact of Ordinals on Bitcoin's Ecosystem

Ordinals represent a significant shift in the Bitcoin ecosystem. Bitcoin was initially designed as a simple, secure, decentralized currency, but the introduction of Ordinals enables it to take on new roles as a platform for digital assets and collectibles. However, this shift brings both positive and negative consequences for Bitcoin's network and its users.

One of the major concerns surrounding Ordinals is that the inscription of large amounts of data (such as images or videos) onto the Bitcoin blockchain could lead to network congestion. Bitcoin's block size is limited, and the addition of NFTs and other large data items may lead to higher transaction fees, as users compete for limited block space.

Some in the Bitcoin community argue that the introduction of NFTs and other non-transactional data onto the blockchain could distract from Bitcoin's core mission of being a decentralized, digital currency. They worry that the increasing use of Bitcoin for non-financial applications may lead to centralization and a departure from Bitcoin's primary role as a store of value.

On the positive side, Ordinals open up new possibilities for Bitcoin, transforming it from a purely financial asset into a platform for digital ownership and collectibles. This could increase Bitcoin's adoption in creative industries and broader digital economies, giving Bitcoin more real-world utility beyond the realm of traditional finance.

The Future of Ordinals

The future of Ordinals is still being shaped, with many questions about how the protocol will evolve and what role it will play in Bitcoin's ongoing development. As the protocol matures, it may inspire the creation of new tools, platforms, and applications that allow users to leverage Bitcoin's decentralized infrastructure for a variety of digital assets and services.

As more inscriptions are added to Bitcoin, scalability may become an issue. Layer 2 solutions like **the Lightning Network** may become increasingly important for handling the additional data load created by Ordinals, as they offer faster and more efficient transactions that could help alleviate congestion on the main Bitcoin blockchain.

As more artists, developers, and creators experiment with Bitcoin NFTs, the demand for Bitcoin-based digital assets may increase. This could lead to the development of marketplaces, exchanges, and platforms specifically tailored for Ordinals, further driving adoption and usage of Bitcoin for non-financial applications.

Ordinals represent a significant development in the evolution of Bitcoin. By allowing the creation of unique, verifiable digital assets directly on Bitcoin's blockchain, the protocol opens up new possibilities for Bitcoin as a platform for digital collectibles, NFTs, and decentralized applications. While challenges remain, particularly concerning scalability and network congestion, the Ordinals protocol has the potential to significantly expand Bitcoin's utility and user base, shaping its role in the digital economy for years to come.

Chapter-29

BRC-20: A New Standard for Tokenization on Bitcoin

Bitcoin, traditionally viewed as a store of value and a digital currency, has recently seen the rise of new protocols and standards that enable the creation of tokens directly on its blockchain. One such standard is **BRC-20**, a token standard built on the **Ordinals protocol** that allows users to create and trade fungible tokens on the Bitcoin network. BRC-20 is often compared to Ethereum's ERC-20 token standard but is native to Bitcoin, using its existing infrastructure without the need for smart contracts.

This chapter explores the BRC-20 standard, how it works, and the impact it has on Bitcoin's ecosystem. We will look into the technical details, potential use cases, and the challenges and opportunities BRC-20 presents for Bitcoin's future as a platform for decentralized finance and tokenization.

What Is BRC-20?

BRC-20 is a token standard built on Bitcoin's **Ordinals protocol** that facilitates the creation of **fungible tokens** on the Bitcoin blockchain. Unlike Ethereum's ERC-20 tokens, which rely on smart contracts for token creation and management, BRC-20 tokens use Bitcoin's existing transaction structure and **JSON-based data** to implement token functionality. This makes BRC-20 a relatively lightweight solution for creating tokens without requiring the deployment of complex smart contracts.

Like other fungible tokens, BRC-20 tokens are interchangeable, meaning each token holds the same value and can be used in place of another. This is in contrast to **non-fungible tokens (NFTs)**, which represent unique assets. As with Ordinals, BRC-20 tokens are inscribed onto individual satoshis, the smallest units of Bitcoin, via the Bitcoin blockchain. These inscriptions store metadata and define the token's properties, including its supply, transfer rules, and other features.

A distinctive feature of BRC-20 is that it does not require the use of smart contracts, which makes it a more straightforward and minimalist solution compared to Ethereum-based token standards. Instead, it relies on Bitcoin's simple transaction format, utilizing the **JSON format** to encode data within the blockchain.

How Does BRC-20 Work?

The BRC-20 standard operates by encoding token-related data directly into Bitcoin transactions through the **Ordinals protocol**. The process involves the following key steps:

The process begins when a user creates a BRC-20 token by inscribing a specific JSON object onto a satoshi. This object defines the token's characteristics, such as the name, total supply, and divisibility (how divisible the token is, similar to how Bitcoin has eight decimal places).

To transfer BRC-20 tokens, users can send Bitcoin transactions that include the relevant inscriptions. Instead of relying on smart contracts or complex script execution, the transfer is executed through simple Bitcoin transactions that carry the token's data along with it.

BRC-20 tokens can be minted (created) and burned (destroyed) by interacting with the Bitcoin blockchain through specially formatted transactions. The minting process involves inscribing tokens onto satoshis, while burning involves removing tokens from circulation by removing the corresponding inscriptions.

JSON format, is a lightweight data-interchange format used widely for transmitting data between servers and applications. The JSON structure holds the essential information about the token, such as its supply, name, and rules for its issuance.

Since the BRC20 standard utilizes Ordinals Protocol each satoshi can be tracked on the blockchain as well.

Several key components define the BRC-20 standard and distinguish it from other tokenization models:

Token Inscription: BRC-20 tokens are inscribed onto Bitcoin's blockchain, specifically onto satoshis, which allows them to be tracked and transferred as part of the Bitcoin transaction history.

Token Rules and Metadata: The core rules of the BRC-20 token, including the total supply, divisibility, and minting rules, are stored as metadata in a JSON object. This object acts as the token's "contract" without the need for a traditional smart contract.

Minting and Burning Mechanisms: The standard allows for the minting and burning of tokens by adding or removing inscriptions on the Bitcoin blockchain. These operations are similar to how Bitcoin's supply is controlled through **proof-of-work** mining but instead utilize transaction data for creating or destroying tokens.

Fungibility and Transferability: Just like other fungible tokens, BRC-20 tokens are interchangeable. Each token has an identical value, and holders can transfer them freely between wallets. The transfer of tokens is done by including the relevant metadata in the transaction output.

Supply and Divisibility: BRC-20 tokens can have a defined total supply and a specified level of divisibility. While Bitcoin is divisible to eight decimal places, BRC-20 tokens can be designed to follow this standard or use a different level of divisibility depending on the project's requirements.

The Advantages of BRC-20

BRC-20 tokens offer several advantages, particularly for users who want to leverage Bitcoin's robust infrastructure while creating fungible tokens. Here are some of the key benefits:

BRC-20 tokens inherit the security and decentralization of the Bitcoin blockchain. Bitcoin's decentralized network and proof-of-work consensus mechanism ensure that BRC-20 tokens are secure, tamper-proof, and resistant to censorship.

Unlike Ethereum's ERC-20 tokens, which require smart contracts for creation and management, BRC-20 tokens are created using Bitcoin's basic transaction structure. This makes the system simpler, less complex, and more lightweight, reducing the potential attack surface and avoiding smart contract vulnerabilities.

The BRC-20 standard takes a minimalist approach, focusing on simplicity and functionality. Its design avoids the complexities associated with other blockchain ecosystems and allows Bitcoin to be used as a more general-purpose platform for tokenization.

Since BRC-20 tokens use Bitcoin's existing infrastructure without the need for complex smart contracts, the transaction fees are typically lower compared to those seen on Ethereum. While the Bitcoin network can experience congestion, BRC-20's reliance on simple transactions can reduce fee volatility.

Despite its advantages, BRC-20 faces several challenges that must be addressed as it evolves:

The Bitcoin blockchain is not optimized for large-scale tokenization. The BRC-20 standard relies on the Bitcoin network's block size and transaction capacity, which can lead to network congestion and higher fees during periods of high demand.

 BRC-20 tokens are limited by Bitcoin's simple transaction structure and lack of native smart contract support. This means that more complex features, such as token staking, governance, or advanced token mechanics, are not directly possible with BRC-20.

The BRC-20 standard is relatively new, and the ecosystem around it is still developing. The lack of robust developer tools, libraries, and infrastructure means that creating and interacting with BRC-20 tokens may be more difficult for developers compared to well-established standards like ERC-20 on Ethereum.

Because BRC-20 tokens use the Bitcoin blockchain for their operations, the increased activity could contribute to network congestion, leading to slower transaction processing times and higher fees. The scalability of the Bitcoin network may become a significant issue as the demand for BRC-20 tokens grows.

The Future of BRC-20

Despite the challenges, BRC-20 has opened up new possibilities for Bitcoin, allowing it to participate in the growing world of decentralized finance (DeFi) and tokenization. The future of BRC-20 tokens will likely involve further innovation and refinement, with several potential developments on the horizon:

Layer 2 solutions, such as the **Lightning Network**, could help alleviate some of the scalability issues associated with BRC-20 tokens by processing token transactions off-chain. This would allow for faster and cheaper transactions while still leveraging the security of the Bitcoin blockchain.

As more developers and projects begin to explore BRC-20, the ecosystem will likely expand, with the development of new tools, wallets, and marketplaces to support the creation and trade of BRC-20 tokens.

As Bitcoin's role in decentralized finance continues to evolve, BRC-20 could serve as a bridge to DeFi applications, enabling Bitcoin to be used in lending, borrowing, and trading without relying on other blockchain ecosystems.

BRC-20 represents an exciting development in Bitcoin's evolution, enabling tokenization and the creation of fungible tokens directly on the Bitcoin blockchain. While it is still in its early stages, BRC-20 holds the potential to expand Bitcoin's use cases, adding a layer of flexibility to Bitcoin's established security and decentralization. As the ecosystem grows and developer tools improve, BRC-20 could become a key part of Bitcoin's future, enabling decentralized finance and expanding Bitcoin's role in the broader digital asset landscape.

That brings an end to the important upgrades. Next, we consider Bitcoin with an economic perspective, various theories surrounding Bitcoin, its price action history and future potential. Theorieeeeessssss here they come!!

Chapter-30

Theories Here They Come

Since its inception in 2009, Bitcoin's been a worthy contender in the financial space, it's a technological marvel and has the power to disrupt traditional financial systems. Bitcoin garnered significant attention from investors, tech enthusiasts, economist and governments.

Bitcoin's aim as a digital currency have been widely accepted, but its other side as a store of value and as "Digital Gold" have been a subject of worldwide debates. From the same a wide array of theories has surfaced to explain and debate Bitcoin's place in the real world, it's price movements and future potential.

That makes it compelling enough to discuss and explore the various Bitcoin theories, ranging from the "digital gold" narrative to Bitcoin as a hedge against inflation or a tool for monetary revolution. Through different lenses we weigh the presence of Bitcoin in this world. I love explanations and perspective from all angles, what about you? You're about to find out!

The Digital Gold Theory

One of the most popular and often debated theories about Bitcoin is the "digital gold" theory. Due to the fixed supply of 21 million, the scarcity and limited supply angle, Bitcoin is often compared to Gold. We cannot deny the fact that the theory is compelling. I mean why not? Both are scarce, difficult to counterfeit, not tied to any single country's economy and decentralized.

The Scarcity angle also competes with fiat currencies. The fact that nobody can mint bitcoin at will makes it attractive as an asset. Sharing the stage with gold strengthens the store of value claim as well. The store of value crown has been given to assets that holds its purchasing power over time, especially in times of economic uncertainty. In an era of rising debt levels, high inflation, and monetary policies that involve quantitative easing (fancy word for printing money), Bitcoin and Gold both have been an attractive option to store your wealth.

Slowly, bitcoin like gold is being considered as a hedge against inflation. We have seen this in effect especially during the COVID 19 pandemic. 2020 was a masterclass on bad monetary policy and an economics 101 year. We had everything, from low interest rates to large scale money printing, and stimulus cheques as well. Bitcoin's growth in the year 2020 and 2021 was parabolic.

Also, much like gold, Bitcoin's value is based on collective belief and perception. Societies have chosen to ascribe value to gold and bitcoin. Bitcoin is stronger than gold when it comes to storage and maintenance charges. Bitcoin has no hidden maintenance and can be stored and moved in a device that fits in your pocket. Even if somebody steals the device, you don't have to run for your money.

Digital Gold theory gave substantial support to Bitcoin and it even made people consider that side of bitcoin rather than their perception of bitcoin as virtual internet money. Some argue that the volatility and short history of Bitcoin does not make it worthy to be classed as an asset or as a store of value. I am leaving it up to you to decide, whose side are you on?

The Store of Value and Wealth Preservation Theory

Derived from the Digital Gold theory is the idea that Bitcoin functions as a store of value for wealth preservation. It states that Bitcoin is the modern-day asset for investors and institutions to preserve their wealth against inflation, currency devaluation and economic instability. It also emphasizes on the consequence of centralized monetary policies.

The theory pulls in real world examples of countries with hyperinflation where its citizen found shelter under Bitcoin. In that sense Bitcoin is a powerful alternative. Bitcoin can be transferred across borders quickly and securely without relying on any intermediary. You can move to any country of your choice with your asset in your pocket. We had the same situation in Venezuela, Argentina and Zimbabwe.

Increasingly, institutional investors and corporations have started adding Bitcoin to their balance sheets. We saw MicroStrategy, Tesla, and of all the institutions BlackRock entered the space with their Bitcoin Exchange Traded Fund (ETF). These big corporations like the fact that Bitcoin is censorship resistant and it takes self-ownership to the next level. No government can freeze a bitcoin wallet, impose capital control during economic unease if you are holding bitcoin in a non-custodial wallet.

The Anti-Inflation Hedge and Safe-Haven Asset Theory

A sibling of the above-mentioned theories and a mixture of both of them, in this theory, Bitcoin is seen as a safe-haven asset, akin to precious metals like gold, that can protect investors against inflationary pressures. Bitcoin's fixed supply of 21 million coins means that no more can ever be created unlike fiat currencies, which can be inflated at will by central banks.

Bitcoin's supply mechanism makes it an attractive hedge during periods of inflation. When the purchasing power of fiat currencies declines, Bitcoin's scarcity and the limited supply become an important feature for investors looking for assets that cannot be devalued through inflationary policies.

Central banks and governments can devalue fiat currencies through policies like quantitative easing, low interest rates, and excessive debt accumulation. In contrast, Bitcoin's supply is fixed, making it immune to such inflationary pressures. For this reason, Bitcoin has been referred to as "digital gold" in the context of its role as a store of value against monetary policy manipulation.

During times of economic crisis, such as the 2008 financial crash or the economic turmoil induced by the COVID-19 pandemic, Bitcoin's decentralized and borderless nature allows it to function as an alternative to traditional financial assets that may be subject to systemic risk. Bitcoin's ability to remain operational without relying on traditional financial infrastructure offers investors a safe-haven asset when confidence in the global financial system wanes.

The Monetary Revolution Theory

Some Bitcoin proponents (me included) believe that Bitcoin is not just an asset but a revolutionary force that could fundamentally change the global financial system. The Monetary Revolution theory suggests that Bitcoin's decentralized nature, its ability to circumvent traditional financial intermediaries, and its role as a censorship-resistant currency could enable it to replace existing forms of money and payment systems.

Bitcoin enables peer-to-peer transactions without the need for intermediaries like banks or payment processors. By cutting out the middleman, Bitcoin reduces transaction fees (the fees for transacting in bitcoin network is same irrespective of the value being sent), increases the efficiency of financial transfers, and creates a more transparent system that is less prone to manipulation by centralized authorities.

Bitcoin gives individuals full control over their own money. Unlike fiat currencies, which can be controlled, manipulated, and devalued by governments, Bitcoin allows users to store their wealth in a decentralized, borderless system. This financial sovereignty is particularly appealing in regions with weak or authoritarian governments, where individuals may face restrictions on their financial freedom.

Bitcoin can be a game-changer for global remittances. Traditional remittance systems, such as Western Union, often charge high fees and take several days for transfers to be completed. Bitcoin allows for instant, low-cost transfers across borders, enabling people to send money to family members or businesses in other countries without relying on expensive intermediaries.

Proponents of this theory believe that as more people and businesses adopt Bitcoin, its role as a global reserve currency or medium of exchange will grow. They envision a world where Bitcoin could eventually replace or coexist with traditional fiat currencies, providing an alternative to the existing monetary system.

The Speculative Asset Theory

While many Bitcoin enthusiasts focus on its utility and potential as a store of value, others view Bitcoin primarily as a speculative asset. According to this theory, Bitcoin's price movements are largely driven by market sentiment, with investors treating Bitcoin as a high-risk, high-reward asset class. This theory places less emphasis on Bitcoin's long-term utility and more on short-term price speculation and market trends.

We cannot deny the fact that Bitcoin's price is highly volatile, with massive price swings occurring in both directions. Speculators believe that by buying at low prices and selling at higher prices, they can profit from Bitcoin's volatility. This speculative behavior has led to significant market bubbles and corrections, which are a defining feature of Bitcoin's price history.

The price of Bitcoin is heavily influenced by investor sentiment, news events, and social media. For example, positive news about institutional adoption or regulatory clarity can lead to price surges, while negative news can trigger sharp declines. Bitcoin's speculative nature makes it an attractive asset for traders who are looking to profit from short-term price movements (I would not advice anyone to do that).

Critics of the store-of-value theory argue that Bitcoin's limited use cases and its inherent volatility make it unsuitable as a long-term store of value. Instead, they view it as a speculative asset whose price is primarily driven by market hype and investor psychology.

Stock-to-Flow (S2F) Model

The Stock-to-Flow model, popularized by the pseudonymous analyst "PlanB," evaluates Bitcoin's scarcity to predict its price. It compares the existing stock (current supply) of Bitcoin to the annual flow (newly mined Bitcoin). As Bitcoin halvings reduce the flow, the stock-to-flow ratio increases, theoretically driving up the price. The model likens Bitcoin to precious metals like gold, emphasizing its scarcity as a value driver. Critics argue that Bitcoin's price is influenced by factors beyond scarcity, such as macroeconomic trends and adoption rates.

Efficient Market Hypothesis (EMH) and Bitcoin

The EMH suggests that all available information is already reflected in Bitcoin's price. This theory implies that predicting Bitcoin's price movements is inherently difficult due to market efficiency.

Strong-form EMH: Price reflects all public and private information.

Weak-form EMH: Price reflects only historical data. Bitcoin's volatile and speculative nature often challenges the notion of efficient pricing.

The Network Effect Theory

This theory states that Bitcoin's value increases as more users adopt it, due to the network effect. The Metcalfe's Law analogy states that the value of a network is proportional to the square of its number of users.

Increased adoption (e.g., businesses accepting Bitcoin, wallet usage) drives utility and, consequently, value. Bitcoin's limited supply coupled with growing adoption supports long-term price appreciation. Adoption alone does not guarantee stable or increasing value, as speculative bubbles can also inflate prices.

Hyperbitcoinization Theory

This theory envisions a future where Bitcoin becomes the dominant global currency, replacing fiat money. It predicts that as confidence in fiat currencies erodes, Bitcoin adoption will accelerate exponentially. Bitcoin's decentralization and deflationary nature make it a superior alternative to inflationary fiat systems. Hyperbitcoinization would lead to a new global monetary standard. But the theory assumes widespread global adoption, which faces significant challenges such as regulatory resistance, technical scalability, and public understanding.

The Bitcoin Trilemma

This theory addresses the trade-offs between decentralization, security, and scalability in blockchain networks. Bitcoin prioritizes decentralization and security over scalability, which has led to challenges like slower transaction speeds and higher fees. Proposed solutions, such as the Lightning Network, aim to improve scalability without compromising Bitcoin's core principles. The trilemma highlights Bitcoin's design philosophy of prioritizing trustlessness and censorship resistance. Critics argue that Bitcoin's scalability issues limit its use as a global payment system.

Austrian Economics and Bitcoin

Rooted in Austrian economics, this theory views Bitcoin as the ultimate form of sound money. It emphasizes Bitcoin's fixed supply, decentralization, and resistance to manipulation by central authorities. Bitcoin aligns with Austrian principles by rejecting inflationary monetary policies. Advocates argue that Bitcoin restores individual sovereignty and protects wealth from government interference. Skeptics question Bitcoin's ability to function effectively as money due to its volatility.

The Lindy Effect

The Lindy Effect suggests that the longer Bitcoin survives, the more likely it is to endure in the future. Each passing year without a critical failure reinforces confidence in Bitcoin's resilience. Bitcoin's robust security and growing adoption support its longevity. The theory encourages long-term investment based on Bitcoin's historical track record. Technological obsolescence or external threats, such as regulatory crackdowns, could disrupt Bitcoin's longevity.

The Miner Capitulation Theory

This theory proposes that periods of extreme price drops force inefficient miners to exit the market, leading to a redistribution of mining power. Such events are often followed by price recoveries as the network stabilizes. Miner capitulation typically occurs during bear markets when mining becomes unprofitable. It is seen as a healthy market correction that strengthens the network. The theory assumes that mining power directly correlates with Bitcoin's price, which is not always the case.

Bitcoin as a Social Movement

This theory views Bitcoin as more than a financial asset, emphasizing its role as a social and political movement. It challenges traditional financial systems and promotes individual freedom through decentralization. Bitcoin empowers individuals by offering an alternative to centralized banking and inflationary policies. The community-driven nature of Bitcoin fosters innovation and resilience. Critics argue that idealistic goals may overshadow practical limitations.

Game Theory in Bitcoin

Bitcoin leverages game theory to align incentives and maintain network security. Miners, nodes, and users participate in a system where cooperation is rewarded, and malicious behavior is penalized. Honest miners are incentivized by block rewards and transaction fees. The decentralized nature ensures no single entity can dominate the network. Centralization trends in mining and governance could challenge the game-theoretic balance.

We have gone through the main theories about bitcoin and I have saved the best one for you as a dedicated chapter. That theory alone shapes the entire crypto market for now.

Drum roll please!!! The Four-Year Cycle.

Chapter -31

Bitcoin and the Four-Year Cycle Theory

The most fascinating and often discussed theory after Area 51 is Bitcoin and its four yearly cycles. The idea of the four-year cycle is your GPS in the world of crypto. It is a theory that still holds and appreciated by the crypto community. I came across this theory while watching a YouTube video. However, I am not entirely sure whether he was the guy behind that theory, so I am not going to take any names here. Only because there is only one thing smaller than a quantum particle; a man's ego!

Where were we, Ahh!! The four-year cycles. These cycles are driven by the Bitcoin halving events (reward cuts into half every 210,000 blocks or roughly 4 years). Let me explain.

We know that the supply is capped at 21 million. A 50% cut decreases the everyday issuance by half. This event usually creates a supply shock in the market. And if the demand is the same and if we cannot meet the supply!! Drum roll.... The price increases, that is economics 101.

And this reduction in supply historically coincided with huge rallies shooting bitcoin's price to outer space!! (That is the moon boy in me talking, the author in me wants to say "the price appreciation is rather appealing to the naked eye).

Don't believe me?

Take a look at this.

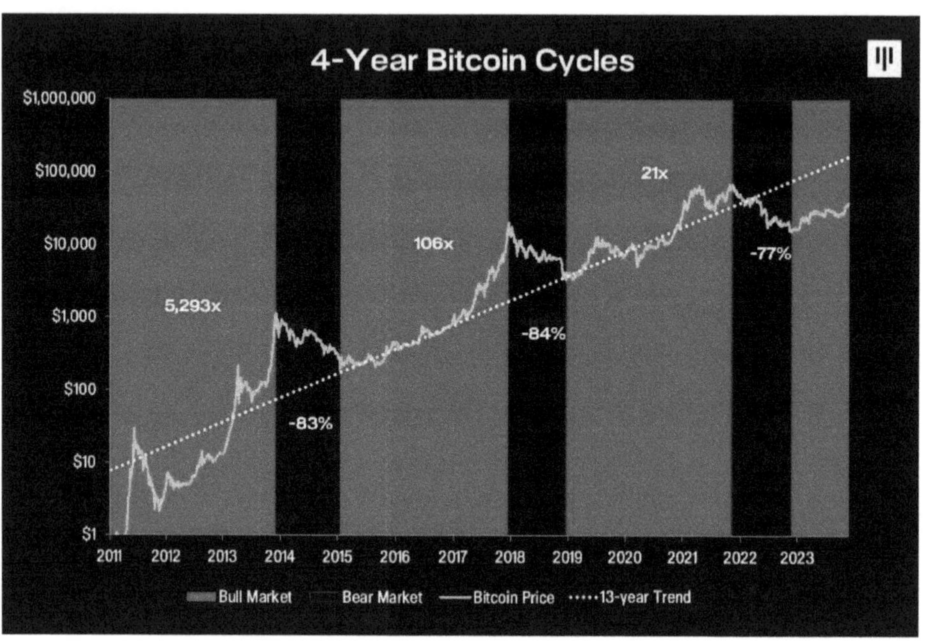

There have been significant price rallies and this follows with a sharp downside as well. Thus, creating a boom-and-bust cycle every four yearly. Generally, 15-18 months after the halving is considered as the parabolic phase.

Till date we had 4 halvings, each had an effect

First Halving (2012): In November 2012, Bitcoin's block reward was halved from 50 BTC to 25 BTC. At the time, Bitcoin's price was still relatively low, trading between $10 and $12. However, the reduced supply over time contributed to a massive price surge, culminating in Bitcoin's first significant bull run, which saw it rise to over $1,100 by the end of 2013.

Second Halving (2016): In July 2016, the reward was halved again, this time from 25 BTC to 12.5 BTC. Bitcoin's price was hovering around $650 at the time, and following the halving, the price began to rise significantly. By the end of 2017, Bitcoin reached its then-all-time high of nearly $20,000.

Third Halving (2020): The third halving took place in May 2020, when the block reward was reduced from 12.5 BTC to 6.25 BTC. Leading up to the halving, Bitcoin's price experienced a dramatic rise, reaching new highs, and in 2021, Bitcoin surged past $60,000, driven by increasing institutional adoption and macroeconomic factors.

Fourth Halving (2024): The most recent halving took place in 19th of April 2024.The block reward was reduced to 3.125 from 6.25. As of now the cycle holds true and every investor and analyst are closely monitoring the cycle.

Each halving event has led to an increase in Bitcoin's price due to the reduction in new supply and the anticipation of scarcity. This creates a supply-demand imbalance, where demand continues to increase as more institutional investors and retail buyers enter the market, driving prices upward. Historically, Bitcoin's bull markets have tended to occur in the year or two following each halving, while the bear markets have followed the peaks.

However, to understand the four yearly cycles we need dissect the cycle and look at each sections carefully. Sharpen you blades!!

The Phases of the Four-Year Cycle

Accumulation Phase (Pre-Halving)

The accumulation face occurs in the years leading up to the halving. Miners continue to mine Bitcoin at a fixed reward rate. During this phase of the cycle the price of Bitcoin moves sideways and relatively stable. The investors and miners know the halving is approaching.

Halvings are usually deadly for miners as their reward is getting cut by half. Most of the small miners shuts of their systems and usually there is a price correction before the halving where these small miners sell off and exit. There are also grapevines about these corrections that the price is **getting manipulated by whales to create panic.**

Bull Market (Post Halving)

Ahh!! The good times. Following the halving, the market feels the greenlight ahead. The halving is not usually priced in. It takes some time for its effect to kick in. First signals are when exchanges run out of bitcoin. The supply shock kicks in and we see the price slowly reacting to it. The upward price pressure increases and we see rapid appreciation in price usually within 15-18 months after halving.

Bitcoin's price has historically reached new all-time highs in the years following the halving. For example, after the 2012 halving, Bitcoin's price surged from around $10 to over $1,100. After the 2016 halving, it went from around $650 to nearly $20,000. In 2021, Bitcoin hit its all-time high of over $60,000, following the 2020 halving.

You feel like a genius, your family and relatives are asking you about Bitcoin. You feel like quitting your job or taking a loan to buy even more bitcoin. You hear a knock on the door, there is your buddy Financial Freedom in a Versace outfit! And while you think about buying the Lambo you dreamt of, the music stops! In the next few days, you see prices plummeting.

Bear Market (Post Bull Market)

After the bull war comes the bloodbath, Bitcoin now has officially entered a bear market phase. We see price falling as much as 80%. This period can last for anywhere between 12-24 months. The market sentiment shifts, we can feel the blood stain in the air around, the bull market days of glory are long gone. Bitcoin retraces back to its previous cycle all-time highs.

During the bear market the people who came for the money sells off fearing further losses, while institutions and whales begins to accumulate Bitcoin at a discount. This phase also sees reduced trading activities and volumes.

Never lose hope, there is always light at the end of the tunnel!!

Accumulation and Preparation for the next cycle:

After the bear market we see the accumulation phase again. The price stabilizes and everybody accumulates bitcoin. Everyone eagerly waits for the next halving event.

Halving has its effect on the price but I don't believe that is the only factor that drives the price. Over the years we have seen institutions adopting bitcoin post halving. We need to take economic conditions into consideration as well. Monetary policy, inflation, geopolitical issues. One of the main examples is during the recent COVID 19 Pandemic many considered Bitcoin as a hedge against inflation creating demand.

It is that page of the chapter where I give you wisdom and advice. Two questions I always get as feedback after I explain Bitcoin to people are Why should I know about all this fancy tech behind bitcoin to invest in it? I don't need to understand how a bank works to use the banking services right?

Fair point!! But in a bull market and that is when most people ask me about bitcoin, you feel like a genius. This is not an exaggeration, that is exactly how you will feel. People act as if they can predict the market. But when the tide retreats and you enter the bear market, when you are having second thoughts about your very interaction with this market, that is when the fundamentals come into the picture.

If you believe in what they created the current price is not a problem. To be on the safer side take profits along the way if you have more exposure to the market. I am not in Bitcoin because of some guy's prediction of 1 million per coin. I am here because of the tech behind bitcoin, and bitcoin has the power to disrupt our traditional system. Money is a by product that came with that belief.

When everything goes south, when the same friends that asked you about bitcoin starts making fun of you, when you are having second thoughts, when you are scared to invest a penny more into bitcoin, when you doubt your very decisions that is when you consider the basics, the fundamentals of Bitcoin and that is when you trust the code and as they say it is **"in code we trust."**

Chapter-32

Bitcoin and the M2 Money Supply: Keep Your Friends Close and Enemies Closer.

While the four yearly cycle emphasizes on the effect of halving, I personally prefer the relation between Bitcoin and M2 money supply. Don't take me wrongly, halving has its own effect in the cycle but I still believe that global liquidity plays a major role in market cycles. Halving is like the engine the heart of Bitcoin it sure propels you forward, but M2 is like the turbocharger which gives that boost, the kick. That is the best analogy I could come up with and it is governments who ease economies, so M2 is definitely a turbo charger and a turbo lag is inevitable.

The M2 money supply represents a broad measure of a nation's money, including cash, checking deposits, and near-money such as savings accounts and time deposits. It is a key indicator of economic activity and liquidity in traditional fiat systems. Bitcoin offers a stark contrast to fiat currency by presenting an alternative monetary system with fixed supply dynamics. Paradoxically, Bitcoin's rise has relied heavily on the very fiat money it aims to disrupt or replace. This chapter explores Bitcoin's connection to the M2 money supply, the implications of its adoption within the fiat-dominated economy, and its potential to transform the global financial landscape.

The M2 money supply is a broad measure of a country's money stock, including:**M1** which is the Physical cash and checking deposits (highly liquid forms of money) and **Near Money** which is the savings accounts, money market accounts, and other deposits that can be quickly converted to cash. Central banks monitor M2 as an indicator of liquidity and economic activity. Expansion of M2 often reflects loose monetary policies, such as those implemented during financial crises or recessions.

The power of minting money in the wrong hands can be fatal to any economy. Over-expansion of M2 can lead to inflation, reducing the purchasing power of fiat money. Historically, unchecked inflation has undermined trust in fiat currencies, creating demand for alternatives like Bitcoin.

As we have discussed earlier, we had quite a lot of cases of hyperinflation in the recent past itself. We as common people should always have a backup incase if everything goes south. In the younger ages an economic issue might be still fatal but we have the energy and time to migrate or restart from scratch. Think about an economic collapse after you have retired or when you are about to retire. This thought always keeps me awake at night and I could never comprehend or even imagine the fact that you worked your whole life to get to a point only to realize that the entire lifetime worth was wiped out in a fortnight. So always and always!!! Have a backup plan.

Everything we do in life is for fiat currencies and fiat currencies, governed by M2, serve as the primary means of acquiring Bitcoin. Rising M2 supplies often correspond with increased liquidity, enabling more investments in Bitcoin and other assets. As central banks expand the M2 supply, concerns over inflation drive investors to seek assets like Bitcoin, gold, and real estate.

The Cantillon Effect describes how money printing disproportionately benefits those closest to the source of new money. Bitcoin offers an alternative system, bypassing traditional gatekeepers and providing equal access to a deflationary asset. And most importantly Bitcoin's price discovery occurs primarily in fiat terms, with major trading pairs denominated in USD, EUR, and other fiat currencies. Institutional adoption of Bitcoin often involves large injections of fiat capital too, further tying Bitcoin's growth to the fiat system.

The speculative nature of fiat markets fuels Bitcoin adoption as investors seeks higher returns in a low-interest-rate environment. The proliferation of fiat money increases capital seeking refuge in alternative assets like Bitcoin. Bitcoin's valuation and liquidity are deeply intertwined with the fiat system it seeks to replace, creating a paradox of dependence.

With all this in mind we still cannot claim that we can replace fiat in the near future. We sure would try hard!!It is pretty hard because bitcoin is still measured in fiat equivalence and not in terms of purchasing power and. Fiat currencies benefit from widespread acceptance and integration into global financial systems. Bitcoin faces challenges in scaling and in adoption to match fiat's ubiquity. Bitcoin's price volatility undermines its role as a stable medium of exchange. Trust in Bitcoin as a reserve asset is growing but remains nascent compared to fiat systems backed by central banks. But having said that we personally would love to see bitcoin as a parallel financial system.

Bitcoin as a Parallel Financial System

Bitcoin offers a decentralized alternative, enabling transactions and wealth storage without reliance on fiat systems. Stablecoins, often pegged to fiat currencies, act as intermediaries between Bitcoin and traditional financial systems, reducing volatility during the transition. As Bitcoin adoption grows, its valuation could increasingly be measured in terms of purchasing power rather than fiat equivalence, reducing dependency on the M2 system.

Monetary easing and M2 expansion create conditions that highlight Bitcoin's deflationary appeal. Economic instability caused by fiat devaluation often accelerates Bitcoin adoption. As Bitcoin gains market share, central banks may face challenges in maintaining trust and stability in fiat systems. The interplay between Bitcoin and fiat systems could evolve into a coexistence model, with Bitcoin functioning as a reserve asset alongside fiat currencies.

We talked about various theories related to Bitcoin cycles. Most prominent among them is the 'Four Year Cycle Theory'. This theory heavily relies on bitcoin halving and the supply shock it creates. Now that is basic economics and I understand that, if demand stays the same and the supply is reduced then hell yeah!! The price should increase. But the effect of the halving should diminish as time passes. I agree that halving from 50BTC to 25 was a major supply shock. But this won't be the same always as we go through more halvings in the future.

Having said all that, the four-year cycle still holds till today in 2024.But in my opinion the M2 money supply has more effect on bitcoin's price action. Have a look at the chart on the next page.

Exhibit 9: Bitcoin market capitalisation growth generally follows M2 money supply growth

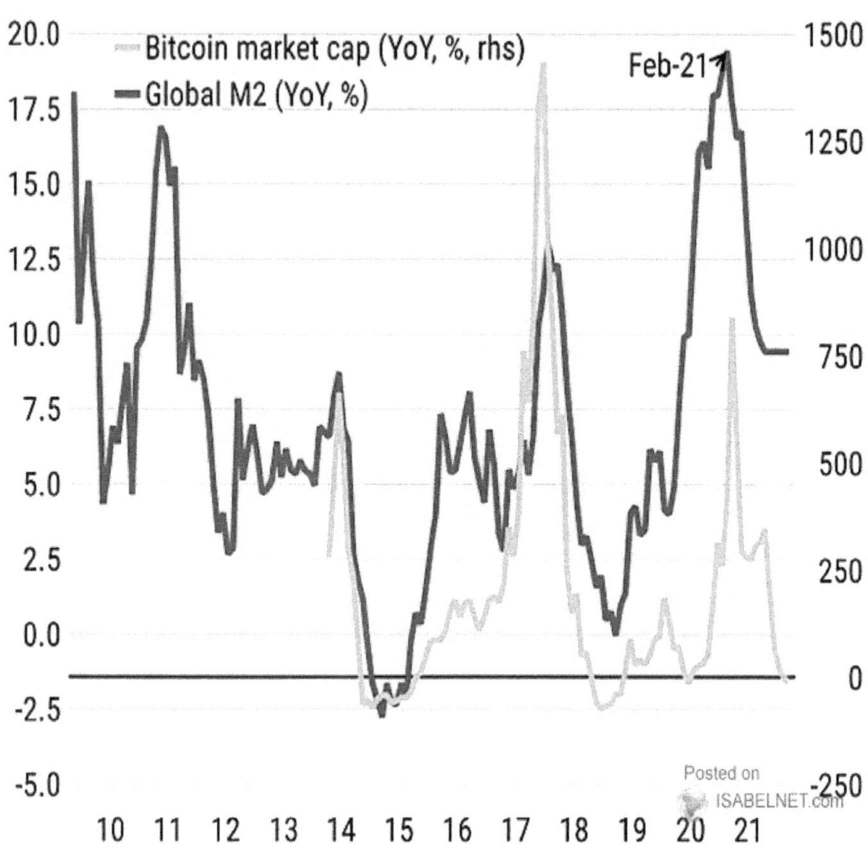

Source: Macrobond, Morgan Stanley Research

The above chart speaks about the correlation. Bitcoin has mirrored the M2 supply till today. And we have to wait to find out what future holds for us. Bitcoin's relationship with the M2 money supply is both adversarial and symbiotic. While Bitcoin seeks to replace fiat currencies, its growth relies on the liquidity and infrastructure provided by the fiat system. This paradox highlights the complexities of transitioning from a centralized monetary framework to a decentralized, deflationary alternative. Understanding this dynamic provides a clearer picture of Bitcoin's role in reshaping the future of money and its potential to fundamentally alter global financial systems.

Chapter-33

Bitcoin vs. Other Assets: The Potential of Bitcoin

Since its inception in 2009 by an anonymous individual or group under the pseudonym Satoshi Nakamoto, **Bitcoin** has emerged as the world's first decentralized digital currency. Over time, Bitcoin has evolved beyond just being a form of money, becoming a significant financial asset and a focal point in the world of digital finance. Bitcoin's uniqueness stems from its decentralized nature, fixed supply, and underlying blockchain technology, all of which contrast sharply with traditional financial assets such as stocks, bonds, and commodities.

As Bitcoin becomes more widely adopted, many are considering how it compares to other major asset classes like global household wealth, gold, real estate, derivatives, and the potential wealth transfer into Bitcoin. Imagine what would happen if just **10% of global wealth** were to shift into Bitcoin.

Global Household Wealth: The Largest Asset Class

Global household wealth represents the sum of assets owned by individuals, including cash, real estate, stocks, and other forms of wealth. According to estimates by institutions like Credit Suisse, global household wealth in 2023 is around **$500 trillion**.

Household wealth is distributed unevenly across the globe, with significant concentration in high-income countries like the United States, Japan, and Western Europe. However, as emerging markets develop, the wealth pool has the potential to increase significantly. Household wealth is typically spread across various asset classes, with real estate and financial assets (stocks, bonds, etc.) making up a significant portion of the total.

 If 10% of global household wealth were to shift into Bitcoin, that would represent a **$50 trillion** influx into the Bitcoin market. Given Bitcoin's current market cap of around **2T** (as of 2024), a 10% wealth transfer would increase its market cap by a factor of roughly 25 times. A $50 trillion influx would propel Bitcoin's market cap to around **$50.6 trillion**, vastly expanding its influence in global financial markets and potentially positioning it as a primary asset class in global portfolios.

The implications of such a massive influx of capital would be profound. Bitcoin would likely become a dominant asset in global finance, potentially overtaking or competing closely with assets like gold and global equity markets.

Bitcoin vs. Gold: The Digital Store of Value

Gold has long been considered a safe-haven asset and a store of value, with a market capitalization estimated to be around **$13 trillion** as of 2024. Bitcoin is often referred to as "digital gold" due to its scarcity (capped at 21 million coins) and its appeal as a hedge against inflation. Gold has been a store of value for thousands of years, especially during times of economic uncertainty. It is used by central banks, investors, and individuals to preserve wealth. Bitcoin shares many similarities with gold, including scarcity and the inability to be inflated by central authorities. However, Bitcoin also offers enhanced portability, divisibility, and security compared to physical gold.

If Bitcoin were to capture 10% of the gold market, that would represent a **$1.3 trillion** influx. This would increase Bitcoin's market cap significantly and bring it closer to **$2 trillion**. And guess what we already did in 2024 Q4!! With the potential for mass adoption, Bitcoin could replace gold as the preferred asset for wealth preservation in the digital age, especially for younger generations and investors seeking easy portability and access to a global, decentralized asset.

While Bitcoin still has a long way to go in terms of adoption and volatility, its scarcity and digital nature make it an increasingly attractive alternative to gold, especially as a hedge against inflation and a store of value in a digitized economy.

Bitcoin vs. Real Estate: A Tangible Asset with Limited Liquidity

Real estate is traditionally one of the largest and most stable asset classes in the world, with a total market capitalization estimated at **$300 trillion** globally. Real estate has long been valued for its ability to provide both a hedge against inflation and a source of rental income. Real estate offers tangible value and utility—whether through ownership of property or income from rental activities. However, real estate markets are highly illiquid, and it is difficult to transfer ownership quickly without the intervention of legal and financial intermediaries.

Bitcoin, by contrast, is highly liquid and can be transferred across borders in seconds, with no need for intermediaries, making it a highly attractive option for investors who seek more flexibility in their wealth management.

If Bitcoin captures just 10% of the global real estate market, that would represent a **$30 trillion** influx into Bitcoin. This would lead to a **$30.6 trillion** Bitcoin market cap, positioning it as a **dominant asset class**.

Bitcoin could revolutionize the real estate industry, enabling fractional ownership, easier cross-border transactions, and more efficient property management, thereby unlocking liquidity in a traditionally illiquid market. While real estate remains a cornerstone of wealth for many, Bitcoin's superior liquidity and portability could disrupt the real estate market, particularly as global investors look for faster and more flexible ways to manage their wealth.

Bitcoin vs. Derivatives: Financial Instruments of Risk

The global derivatives market is enormous, with an estimated **$1.2 quadrillion** in notional value. Derivatives are financial contracts whose value is derived from an underlying asset, such as stocks, bonds, commodities, or currencies. While derivatives themselves are not "assets" in the traditional sense, they play a major role in global finance.

Derivatives are primarily used for hedging and speculation, allowing investors to manage risk in their portfolios. However, they can also contribute to financial instability due to the complexity of some contracts and their potential to create excessive leverage. As Bitcoin becomes more recognized as a store of value and hedge against inflation, it could replace certain derivative products (like inflation-linked bonds or currency hedges) as a primary tool for managing risk.

If Bitcoin were to capture even a small portion of the derivatives market, say 10%, that would represent an influx of **$120 trillion** into Bitcoin. This would push Bitcoin's market cap to **$120.6 trillion**, making it a significant player in the world of financial derivatives and risk management.

Bitcoin's role in this context is still in its early stages, but as more institutional investors adopt Bitcoin as a hedge and as tools for derivative-like products based on Bitcoin emerge, its potential within global financial markets could expand significantly.

What Would 10% of Global Wealth in Bitcoin Look Like?

Taking the above market caps into account, let's explore the cumulative impact of 10% of global wealth being transferred into Bitcoin:

- **Global Household Wealth**: $50 trillion
- **Gold Market**: $1.3 trillion
- **Real Estate Market**: $30 trillion

- **Derivatives Market**: $120 trillion

Total potential wealth inflow into Bitcoin = **$201.3 trillion**.

If just 10% of these assets were shifted into Bitcoin, it would increase Bitcoin's market cap by a staggering **$201 trillion**, bringing Bitcoin's total market cap to **$201.9 trillion**.

This is approximately **four times the total market cap** of all global stocks combined and over 10 times the market cap of all gold. At this scale, Bitcoin would not just be a digital asset; it would be the dominant asset in the global financial system, eclipsing other assets and potentially becoming the reserve currency of the future.

The potential of Bitcoin is vast when considering the massive market caps of traditional asset classes such as global household wealth, gold, real estate, and derivatives. The idea of 10% of global wealth flowing into Bitcoin is not an outlandish scenario given Bitcoin's increasing acceptance among institutional investors and the growing demand for decentralized assets.

If Bitcoin were to capture even a fraction of these massive pools of wealth, its market cap would skyrocket, positioning it as a dominant asset class and reshaping the global financial system.

Good Bye & All the Best

As I bring this journey to a close, I am overwhelmed by a mix of emotions. Writing about Bitcoin is not merely an exploration of technology or economics—it is a deep personal odyssey into a vision that has changed the world forever. At the heart of it all lies the enigmatic figure of Satoshi Nakamoto.

Satoshi's creation was more than code; it was a statement—a challenge to centuries-old systems of control, trust, and value. The anonymity of Satoshi amplifies their brilliance, allowing the idea to transcend the person. For me, Satoshi is not just a creator but a symbol of selflessness and innovation, someone who gifted humanity with a tool so transformative that it defies categorization. Their absence reminds us that Bitcoin belongs to no one and to everyone at once.

Bitcoin represents the first asset in human history that offers 100% ownership. No intermediary, no bank, no authority can lay claim to your wealth if it resides on the Bitcoin network. This profound shift gives power back to the individual, where it has always belonged. For centuries, we have been accustomed to relinquishing control in exchange for trust in centralized entities. Bitcoin erases that dependency, restoring sovereignty and freedom in ways previously unimaginable.

For those living under oppressive regimes, for the unbanked, for anyone who has ever faced the fragility of traditional financial systems, Bitcoin is more than a currency—it is a lifeline. It's a backup plan in times of turmoil, a safety net when trust erodes, and a powerful tool for ensuring that value endures beyond borders, institutions, or lifetimes.

But Bitcoin is not perfect, nor is it a panacea. It is a tool, and like any tool, its power lies in how we choose to use it. The responsibility rests on all of us—to educate, to innovate, and to ensure that this profound invention is wielded to build a better, more equitable future.

As I reflect on this journey, I realize that Bitcoin is not just about money; it's about hope. It's about the idea that we can build systems that empower the individual without sacrificing the collective good. It's about trustless systems that inspire trust in humanity. It's about a future where value is no longer dictated but discovered, shared, and preserved by all.

Satoshi's vision ignited a revolution, but the revolution is far from over. It is now our responsibility to carry that torch, to safeguard the ethos of decentralization and freedom, and to ensure that Bitcoin fulfills its promise as a tool of empowerment for generations to come.

The relation to M2 money supply still gives me goosebumps. I truly believe that Satoshi was a computer scientist, a mathematician, an economist, a person who worked in the financial field and a true visionary. Most of the governments have tried stopping and even banning Bitcoin. It still lives to fight another day. And what does it use as fuel? The same fiat currencies it was designed to replace. Keep your friends close and enemies closer. If that ain't a motivation then what is!!!.

In Bitcoin, I see a reflection of our collective potential—our ability to innovate, to question, and to strive for something greater. And for that, I am deeply grateful.

To Satoshi, wherever you are: thank you. Your legacy is a beacon, a reminder that even in anonymity, one person—or perhaps a group—can change the world. Bitcoin is your gift to humanity, and it is up to all of us to honor it.

And as they say ***in code we trust!! chao!***

# #

51% Attack An attack on blockchain by a group of miners controlling more than 50% of network hash rate

A

Address Delegation of a wallet's stake to a Super Staker

Airdrop A way to promote cryptocurrencies by sending some free tokens to traders

Algorithm: Algorithm is a set of rules to follow to solve a problem or conduct a task.

Algorithmic Stablecoin: Algorithmic stablecoins are tokens pegged to a fiat currency which is usually the US dollar, purely through software and specific conditions.

All-Time-High (ATH): The highest point (in price, in market capitalization) that a cryptocurrency has been in history.

All-Time-Low (ATL): The lowest point (in price, in market capitalization) that a cryptocurrency has been in history.

Altcoin: Coins alternative to Bitcoin

Application Programming Interface (API): It is a software that acts like an intermediary or a bridge that lets two applications talk to each other. It is the one that lets applications, data and devices interact.

Application-Specific Integrated Circuit (ASIC): Refers to specialized computers that are made to do a very specific task (eg. calculate hashes for Bitcoin's Proof-of-Work)

Arbitrage: A strategy where investors buy a currency in a market and sell it at a higher price in another market to gain profit.

ASIC Resistant: A term used to describe cryptocurrency proof-of-work protocols that are resistant to Application-Specific Integrated Circuit (ASIC), by packing in various parameters that make it difficult for ASICs to have a competitive edge against consumer hardware.

Atomic SWAP: Atomic Swap refers to the exchange of cryptocurrencies that operate in different block chains without intermediaries.

Automatic Replay Protection: Automatic Replay Protection refers to the upgrade implemented by Bitcoin Cash to stop the loss of funds from exchanges through replay attacks.

B

Bagholder: A person who is holding a large quantity of cryptocurrency which is declining in value or becoming worthless

Batch Auction: A Batch Auction distributes a number of tokens to users that is proportional to their contribution to the pool.

Bearish: A term used to indicate negative sentiment towards the market or an asset, where investors believe that there will be downward price movement.

Bear Market: Contrary to bull market, it indicates the direction of the market going for downward trend.

Bitcoin ATM: A machine from which you can buy or sell Bitcoin. Typically, also offers different types of cryptocurrencies.

 Bitcoin Evangelist: Individuals who are passionate about Bitcoin, and are dedicated in spreading knowledge about Bitcoin

Bitcoin Improvement Proposal (BIP): Refers to improvement proposals for Bitcoin, used to introduce features or any updates on the Bitcoin network.

BitLicense: Refers to the business license issued by the New York State Department of Financial Services (NYSDFS) to companies dealing with Cryptocurrencies (subject to certain exceptions) in New York.

Block: In the context of blockchain, block refers to the collection of transactional data or information that are bundled together in a predetermined size.

Blockchain: In Bitcoin's case, blockchain describes its decentralized, public ledger which contains transactional information.

 Block Confirmation: Refers to the number of confirmations a particular block has. Each block ahead of the referenced block adds one block confirmation to it.

Block Explorer: Application or websites which display information such as status of transactions or data contained in a block of a given public blockchain network.

Block Height: A number that is used to indicated the position of a particular block within a blockchain

Block Reward: One of the mechanisms built into a blockchain to incentivize validators

Bloodbath: In context of trading, the term bloodbath is commonly used to describe a market which is on a downtrend with many assets suffering from value depreciation.

 Bots: Refers to software or programmes that automatically trade based on preset behaviours.

Bounty: Public tasks available for anyone for a reward

BUIDL: An advice for investors to contribute new projects on blockchain rather than holding cryptocurrencies and waiting for the price to increase

Bullish: A term used to indicate positive sentiment towards the market or an asset, where investors believe that there will be upward price movement.

Bull Market: A bull market indicates the direction of the market going in an upward trend.

Burned Tokens: Tokens which have been sent to addresses whose private key are not known, effectively becoming unusable.

Buy/Sell Tax: On-chain buy or sell tax rate where a percentage of the tokens bought/sold will be transferred to a set address.

Buy Wall: Anomalously large buy order(s) at a single price point that reflects as a "wall" in the order book.

Byzantine Fault: A byzantine fault is where an error has occurred, yet a computer system does not know due which component/what failed to the lack of information and continues to iterate on a given instruction.

Byzantine Generals' Problem: A term used to describe the situation a single strategy which requires consensus from all members within a group who cannot be trusted or verified

C

cco NFT: A cco NFT is a piece of digital content where the IP rights have been relinquished.

Central Bank Digital Currency (CBDC): It is a digital fiat currency issued by the central banks, contrary to cryptocurrency that issued by non-legislative party.

Centralized: An organization structure wherein a small handful of actors have control over the entire network.

Circulating Supply: An approximation of the number of coins or tokens that are currently not locked and available for public transactions.

Cloud Mining: Mining on blockchains through rented processing power rented from companies that host the physical equipment.

Cold Storage: Offline storage of cryptocurrencies which is arguably safer as they also require physical access (eg. hardware wallet, paper wallets)

Cold Wallet: Wallets that are offline and require physical access to certain devices (eg. hardware wallet, paper wallets)

Composability: Composability refers to the ability to combine different components of a software stack.

Consensus: Consensus is achieved in a blockchain system when all participants agree on the content of the next block that will be added onto the blockchain.

Crowdsale: This type of auction has a fixed price per token that is sold on a first-come-first-serve basis.

Crypto Bubble: It is a speculation in the cryptocurrencies and the price of cryptocurrencies would go extremely high before the bubble bursts.

Cryptocurrency: A form of digital currency that utilizes cryptographic protocols to record ownership and prevent counterfeiting

 Cryptography: A discipline or field of study which practices using cryptography to convert human-readable information that can only be deciphered by individuals who have the knowledge to.

Custody: Protective care or guardianship of an asset.

D

Daily Active Addresses (DAA): On a blockchain, users interact with one another through their addresses, and daily active addresses (DAA) refers to the number of addresses which fulfils the defined activity parameter on a given blockchain.

Dead Cat Bounce: Price rally that is short lived after a prolonged decline. Price charts will show a recovery in anticipation of a market turnaround only to decline further.

 Decentralized: A system where there are no centralized points of failure or organization with no central authority figure.

Decentralized Applications (dApps): Applications that run on decentralized peer-to-peer networks such as Ethereum.

Decentralized Autonomous Organization (DAO): Open source and decentralized systems that do not require centralized operators or controllers.

Decentralized Finance (DeFi): Decentralized Finance (DeFi) refers to the movement of building decentralized financial applications that have no central authority and is censorship free.

Decryption: The process of decrypting data that was previously encrypted (made unreadable) back to a readable form.

Degen: Crypto trading without Due Diligence and research - basically gambling

Derivatives: A financial instrument which derives its value from the performance of an underlying asset or index (eg. gold, crude oil)

Derivatives Market: A market for derivatives which are instruments such as futures or options whose value is derived from an underlying asset.

Difficulty: A relative measure on how difficult it is to correctly guess a new block

Directed Acyclic Graph (DAG): Directed acyclic graphs refers to a data structure that is built in one single direction, yet branches out and never repeats.

Distributed Denial of Service (DDoS) Attack: A common cyber-attack tactic where a perpetrator diverts large amounts of traffic towards a particular network or service in an effort to disrupt normal services.

Distributed Ledger: Ledgers whose data is stored and synced across a network of nodes.

Distributed Ledger Technology (DLT): Describes the technology that enables distributed ledger.

Dominance: Typically refers to Bitcoins' market capitalization dominance.

Double Spending: Double spending refers to the act of spending digital currencies twice. This is most commonly applied on crypto exchanges by unscrupulous actors.

Dump: A common term used to describe downward market movement, or to describe the action of selling an individual's holdings.

Dusting Attack: A new form of malicious activity in which hackers and scammers attempt to undermine the privacy of cryptocurrency users by sending little amounts of money to their wallets.

Dutch Auction: A Dutch Auction, also known as an "inverted" auction, starts off with high asking price that decays over time until a pre-determined floor price.

E

EIP (Ethereum Improvement Proposal): Refers to improvement proposals for Ethereum, used to introduce features or any updates on the Ethereum network.

Emission: The speed/rate at which new coins are minted and released as dictated by the protocols written.

Encryption: In cryptography, encryption is a process of encoding information the original form of information called plaintext via an algorithm called cipher. The encrypted message is now called ciphertext. Only authorized parties can decipher the ciphertext and convert back it to the original plaintext.

Enterprise Ethereum Alliance (EEA): Enterprise Ethereum Alliance is made up for a group of Ethereum developers, corporations as well as startups who are collaborating to find ways to use Ethereum for business applications.

ERC-1155: ERC-1155 token standard allows each token ID to represent both non-fungible (NFTs) and fungible tokens which may have their metadata, token supply and other attributes.

ERC-20: ERC-20 is one of the most widely used token standards in Ethereum to create fungible, exchangeable tokens.

ERC-721: ERC-721 is one of the most widely used token standards in Ethereum to create non-fungible, exchangeable tokens.

Ethereum Name Service (ENS): Ethereum Name Service (ENS) is a look-up service that allows Ethereum users to find websites or send and receive funds via simple names.

Ethereum Virtual Machine (EVM): Ethereum Virtual Machine (EVM) is the environment in which all smart contracts are executed.

Exchange Traded Fund (ETF): An exchange-traded fund (ETF) is a form of security that tracks a collection of securities such as stocks, bonds, index or cryptocurrency but tradeable like a single stock.

Explain Like I'm Five (ELI5): To explain in such simple terms that even a five-year-old would be able to understand it.

Externally Owned Accounts (EOA): Externally owned accounts (EOAs) are accounts that are controlled by a private key and have no coding associated with them.

F

Faucet: A faucet usually represents a site or app where a user can navigate to for small rewards repeated over time.

Fear of Missing Out (FOMO): Refers to the feeling of apprehension for missing out on a potentially profitable investment opportunity and regretting it later. Generally, an expression describing investors' fear of missing out the good timing of buying cryptocurrencies that could eventually be profitable

Fear, Uncertainty and Doubt (FUD): A strategy to dissuade people from buying a particular cryptocurrency by spreading false information

Fiat-Pegged Cryptocurrency: Cryptocurrencies are pegged to an underlying asset.

Flappening: Flappening is a term used to describe Litecoin growing bigger and becoming more valuable than Bitcoin Cash (BCH). It is spawned from the term Flippening (used when another crypto overtakes Bitcoin).

Frontrun: To intercept a particularly large AMM, buy order for the purpose of purchasing a reselling the assets back to the buyer before the order transaction is mind on the blockchain.

Full Node: Full Nodes are computers that verify the set of rules that are built into the protocols of a given cryptocurrency.

Full Pay-Per-Share (FPPS): FPPS is quite similar to PPS; the only difference is that the pool will additionally pay a transaction fee incentive if the block is identified. FPPS is the same as PPS+.

Fully Diluted Valuation: Fully Diluted Valuation (FDV) is the theoretical market capitalization of a coin if the entirety of its supply is in circulation, based on its current market price. The FDV value is theoretical as increasing the circulating supply of a coin may impact its market price. Also depending on the tokenomics, emission schedule or lock-up period of a coin's supply, it may take a significant time before its entire supply is released into circulation.

Futures: An agreement between two counterparties that obligates them to transact in the future based on the contract terms set.

G

Gas: A unit of measurement of the computational effort in conducting transactions or smart contracts on Ethereum blockchain.

Gas Limit: A term refers to the maximum number of units of gas user's willingness to spend on a transaction on Ethereum blockchain.

Gas Price: A term refers to the amount of price user is willing to pay for a transaction on Ethereum blockchain.

Genesis Block: It is the first block of data that is processed and validated to form a new blockchain, typically called as 'block 0' or 'block 1'.

Golden Cross: It is a bullish signal in technical candlestick pattern by comparing two lines of short-term moving average and long-term average. It is a golden cross when the short-term moving average broke its long-term moving average.

Gwei: The monetary domination of gas, involving Ether

H

Halving: Event that serves to reduce in half the reward of the Proof-of-Work miners that operate in the blockchain network.

Hard cap: The maximum amount that an ICO will be raising.

Hard Fork: It is a permanent divergence of a blockchain into two blockchains. The original blockchain does not recognize the new version.

Hash: A hash function is an output code (unique and alphanumeric) that we obtain from an input string,

Hashgraph: Hashgraph is a distributed ledger system that has been compared to the blockchain idea as a continuation or successor.

 Hashrate: Total processing power of a blockchain or what is the same, are the amount of hash values that can be made in a period of time.

HODL: A crypto slang of saying holding the assets rather than selling it. A crypto slang encouraging investors to hold on to their assets rather than selling it.

Hot Wallet: It is a tool that store your cryptocurrencies and always connected to internet

Hyperledger (Hyperledger Foundation): Hyperledger is an open-source collaborative effort to create blockchain technologies hosted by The Linux Foundation since 2016.

I

IEO: Initial Exchange Offering (IEO) is a spin-off of Initial Coin Offering (ICO), where the sale of tokens is conducted on an exchange rather than by the coin team themselves.

Immutable: A property characterized by inability to be change and stays unchanged over time.

Impermanent Loss: Temporary loss of funds due to volatility leading to divergence in price between token pairs provided by liquidity providers.

Initial Coin Offering (ICO): Initial Coin Offering (ICO) is the equivalent of Initial Public Offering (IPO), where a company/cryptocurrency venture raises funds through crowd sales.

Internet of Things (IoT): It is a system that lets any devices that are connected to internet to communicate with each other without human-to-human or human-to-devices interactions.

Interoperability: Interoperability refers to the property of product/systems that are able to work with products/systems that are different without any restrictions.

InterPlanetary File System (IPFS): The InterPlanetary File System (IPFS) is a peer-to-peer network and distributed file system protocol for storing and transferring data.

K

Kimchi Premium: The kimchi premium is the price difference between South Korean exchanges and other global exchanges for bitcoin.

KYC (Know Your Customer): KYC stands for "Know Your Customer", a process for business entities is required to verify its clients and assessing them.

L

Ledger: A record of financial transactions that cannot be changed, only appended with new transactions.

Lightning Network: It is the "second layer" or an off-chain of payment protocol that operates on top of a blockchain. Payments on this network do not need block confirmation and it will be instant.

Limit Order / Limit Buy / Limit Sell: Orders placed by traders to buy or sell a cryptocurrency when a certain price is reached

Liquidity: The ease of which cryptocurrency can be bought and sold without impacting the overall market price.

M

Mainnet: It is the main network of Bitcoin, where the transactions of this cryptocurrency are registered and take place.

Margin Call: Margin call takes place when investor's margin account falls below the required amount to stay afloat.

Margin Trading: It is a way of investing by borrowing money from a broker (or in crypto, an exchange or platform) to trade

Market capitalization (market cap): In Crypto, market cap is measured by multiplication of the circulating supply of tokens or currency and its current price

Market Maker: Participant of the market who creates buy and orders

Market Order / Market Buy / Market Sell: A market order is a buy or sell order of stocks or cryptocurrency at the best price available in the current market as soon as possible.

Market Taker: Participant of the market who buys and sells from currently existing orders

Masternodes: Computers that are responsible for processing blockchain transactions and receive a reward when a block is mined.

Mempool: It is the abbreviation of Memory Pool. Set of unconfirmed transactions in a blockchain

Merkle Tree: A Merkle tree is also known as a hash tree in cryptography. It is a tree where every lead node is labelled with cryptographic hash of a data block, and every non-leaf node is labelled with the hash of the labels of its child nodes. It is used to verify of data stored within it and transferable in and between computers.

Metaverse: The Metaverse is a virtual space where users are able to interact with each other in a computer-generated environment.

MicroBitcoin (uBTC): One millionth of a bitcoin or 0.000001 of a bitcoin. Microbitcoin is the abbreviation of uBTC and often misunderstood as the fork of Bitcoin.

Mineable: A cryptocurrency is said to be "mineable" when it has the system through which miners can be rewarded with newly-created cryptocurrencies for creating blocks.

Miners: Contributors to a blockchain taking part in the process of mining.

Mining: It is the process of the miners verify and adding transaction records into a block.

Mining Contract: Another term for cloud mining, where users can rent or invest in mining capacity online.

Mining Pool: Combination of resources of several miners to obtain a higher mining power and thus achieve greater rewards for the opening of blocks.

Mining Reward: The reward resulting from contributing computing resources to process transactions

Mining Rig: A dedicated hardware to mine

 Mnemonic Phrase: A mnemonic phrase (also known as mnemonic seed, or seed phrase) is a list of words used in sequence to access or restore your cryptocurrency assets.

Moon: "Moon" or "To the moon" is a crypto slang that describes an exclamation when the cryptocurrencies prices are rising and when it hit the peak, the coin is said to be "mooning".

Mt. Gox: Mtgox or Mt. Gox was one of the first websites where users could take part in fiat-to-bitcoin exchange (and vice versa).

Multisignal (multi-signature): They are wallets that require more than one key for transactions to be authorized.

N

Node: Within the blockchain network, the nodes are computers that connect to the network and have an updated copy of the blockchain

Nonce: Abbreviation for 'number only used once' It is of vital importance next to the hash in the verification of data from the Bitcoin blockchain network.

Non-custodial: It is a decentralized type-of-wallet, where the users own the private keys.

Non-Fungible Tokens (NFT): They are collectible elements within the Ethereum blockchain under ERC-721, where each token refers to a single element with a certain value

O

Off-chain: It refers to transactions occurring outside the blockchain and executed instantly.

Offline Staking: Staking without needing to be connected to the blockchain

Open/Close: The price at which a cryptocurrency opens at a time period, for example at the start of the day; the price at which a cryptocurrency closes at a time period, for example at the end of the day.

Open Source: Open-source software is a type of software released under a license in which the copyright holder grants users the rights to study, change, and distribute the software to anyone and for any purpose.

Oracles: In the context of crypto, oracles refer to services which verify real-world and provide data to blockchains/smart **contracts.**

Order Book: An electronic list of all buys and sells orders in an exchange

Over The Counter (OTC): It refers to the process that cryptocurrencies are being traded outside exchange and it is done directly between two parties

P

Pay-Per-Last N Shares (PPLNS): PPLNS system only pays miners after the pool has discovered the block. This means you'll only be compensated once the block has been discovered.

Pay-Per-Share (PPS): You are compensated for each valid share that you contribute. Each share is worth a set amount of cryptocurrency that may be mined.

Peer to Peer: A communication protocol that does not require a central hub

Permissioned Blockchain: It is a private blockchain where the nodes must be previously authorized by a central entity.

Ponzi Scheme: A Ponzi scheme is also referred to as pyramid scheme, and typically takes the form of an investment scheme which pays existing investors with funds collected from new investors.

Portfolio: A portfolio consists all of your current crypto holdings in one place.

Pre-sale: A typically exclusive token sale event preceding a public ICO

Privacy Coins: Cryptocurrencies that are designed with transaction anonimity and user privacy in mind.

Private Keys: The alphanumeric string which allows transactions from the cryptocurrency address

 Protocol: The set of rules in a network in which participating members comply to allow proper communication.

Public Blockchain: An open sourced blockchain where participation is public and permissionless

Public Keys: The alphanumeric string which serves as a public receiving address in cryptocurrencies.

Pump and Dump Scheme: A market manipulation method to drive up the price of an asset before profiting by driving it back down.

Q

QR Code: Abbreviation "Quick Response Code", QR code is a machine-readable optical label that stores up to 3Kb of data

R

REKT: A shorthand slang for "wrecked", typically describes bad trades that results in losses.

Replay Attack: A replay attack is a form of network attack when valid data transmission is fraudulently intercepted, then delayed or resent to mislead the receiver into doing what the hacker wants.

Ring Signature: A type of digital signature performed in a group where it becomes impossible to determine which member's key in the group were used for the digital signature.

ROI: Short for "Return on Investment", the ratio between the net profit and cost of investing.

Rug Pull: Sudden removal of liquidity which typically leads to asset prices crashing from the lack of liquidity to absorb buy/sells.

S

Salt (cryptography): In cryptography, a salt is the additional random input that is added to password or passphrase to make the password hash unique. It prevents from the hashed output password to be cracked so easily by the hacker.

Satoshi: A unit measure for the smallest divisible unit of a bitcoin. 1 bitcoin is equal to 100 million Satoshi.

Satoshi Nakamoto: The pseudonym used in publishing the Bitcoin Whitepaper. Identity is unknown.

Scrypt: one of the hashing algorithms used in proof-of-work protocol, Scrypt requires more memory in order to performing mining functions

Second-Layer Solutions: Secondary network or framework built atop an existing blockchain to address transaction speed and scalability issues.

Secure Asset Fund for Users (SAFU): A feature created by Binance which contains reserve funds that can be used to reimburse users in case of a catastrophic event (eg. exchange hack)

Seed: A value used to initiate generation of pseudorandom number, usually a string of 12 common English words.

Segregated Witness (SegWit): A soft fork implementation to change the Bitcoin Protocol's transaction format to address Bitcoin's scalability issues whilst introducing new features.

Sell wall: Anomalously large sell order(s) at a single price point that reflects as a "wall" in the order book.

SHA-256: Abbreviation of "Secure Hashing Algorithm - 256", SHA-256 is part of the SHA2 that allows one-way hashing of any data into a 64-character string.

Sharding: A form of database partitioning which breaks up data into smaller segments.

 Shilling: One who poses as a enthusiastic customer to swindle others as a form of covert advertising.

Shitcoin: A coin with no obvious potential value or usage.

Side Chain: A separate blockchain ledger that runs parallel with the primary blockchain.

Smart contracts: Self-executing contracts on the blockchain without needing human executors or notary.

Soft Cap: Targeted fund-raising limit of an ICO

Soft Fork: A backward-compatible update to a decentralized blockchain protocol.

Software Development Kit (SDK): It is a collection of software development tools in one package installation. It is designed to help developing applications for a specific device or operating system (OS).

Solidity: Object oriented programming language used in various smart contract blockchains.

Solo Staker: A Qtum PoS miner using their own coins for staking. Qtum blockchain launched with Solo Stakers and will continue to have this available after offline staking launches.

Stablecoin: Cryptocurrency with a price peg to fiat currencies or commodity.

Staking: The state of locking-in significant amount of token to participate as a validator of a Proof-of-Stake network.

Stale Block: Double mined blocks that are not included in the blockchain.

State Channel: Secondary payment channel occurring off-chain

STO: Security Token Offering (STO) refers to a public offering for tokenized digital securities, or in short security tokens traded in cryptocurrency exchanges.

Stop-loss Order: Conditional market order to sell at the next available price, executed if the price of an asset falls below set-upon limit

T

Tangle: The name for IOTA's Directed acylic graph (DAG) based transaction settlement layer.

Testnet: Shorthand for "Test Network", testnets are staging areas for experimenting new blockchain features.

Ticker: A ticker is a stock or asset symbol that abbreviates the asset name and it can be used as an identifier of the asset.

Token: Blockchain based unit of value issued by an organization, which grants token holders a right to participate in a network.

Token Burn: An event in which tokens are verifiably removed permanently removed from circulation.

Token Generation Event (TGE): An event in which new tokens (usually on a smart contract platform) are created and distributed to the public.

Total Supply: All the tokens and coins that will exist in a cryptocurrency network.

Total Value Locked: Total Value Locked (TVL) represents the number of assets that are currently staked in a protocol or the total quantity of underlying amount of funds that a DeFi protocol has secured.

Trading Volume: The amount of the cryptocurrency that has been traded in the last 24 hours.

 Transaction Fee: A payment to the network for performing a transaction to be recorded on the blockchain.

Trustless: Entirely verifiable, without needing to trust or assume an **action is done completely and in good faith.**

Turing-Complete: A "turing complete" code or blockchain refers to the ability to read program-written codes.

U

Unspent Transaction Output: (Abbv. "UTXO") Coins that are unspent in the wallet. UTXO virtually represents the cryptocurrency one own in the wallet.

Utility Token: cryptocurrency tokens with specific utilities on a network besides being used as medium of exchange and investment vehicle.

V

Validator: A block-signing participant of a Proof of Stake blockchain network, whom have significant tokens staked on the network.

Variable Buy/Sell Tax: On-chain buy sell tax rate that is not fixed, whereby it is possible for contract owners to change at will.

Venture Capital: capital (funds) that is invested in a company that needs a substantial pool of funds to initiate.

Virtual AMM (vAMM): The vAMM functions similarly like an AMM but does not contain an actual asset pool.

W

Wallet: Software client that handles storage of cryptocurrencies and allows users to send cryptocurrencies.

Wallet Address: The address in which cryptocurrency can be stored, sent to and receive.

Web3 Wallet: Web3 Wallet is the software that allows you to interact with web 3.0.

Wei: The smallest fraction of an Ether, with each Ether to 1000000000000000000 Wei.

Whale: Someone who holds an enormous amount of cryptocurrency and has the ability to wave the market

When Lambo: An expression used by investors to ask when the value of their investment could buy them a Lamborghini

When Moon: An expression used by investors to ask when the price of a coin would hit a peak

Whitelist: List of approved participants that will be given access to a token sale (ICO, IEO, STO etc...)

Whitepaper: An introductory paper to concisely explain an issue and a possible solution on the issue.

Y

Yield Farming: Yield farming involves putting cryptocurrency into a DeFi protocol to collect interest on trading fees.

YTD: Acronym for Year-to-date

Z

Zero Confirmation Transaction: Another name for "unconfirmed transaction"

Zero Knowledge Proof: Cryptographic proof for 2 parties to verify a value without revealing what the value is.

Zero-Knowledge Succinct Non-Interactive Argument of Knowledge (Zk-Snarks): An acronym for Zero-Knowledge Succinct Non-Interactive Argument of Knowledge, zk-SNARKs refers to a protocol where one can prove possession of a given piece of information (e.g. a string or hash) without revealing that information and also without any interaction between both the prover & verifier.

zkML (Zero-Knowledge Machine Learning): Zero-Knowledge Machine Learning (zkML) integrates the principles of zero-knowledge proofs with ML.

zkOracle: zkOracle is an advanced concept in blockchain technology that combines the properties of oracles with the principles of zero-knowledge proofs.

Although it contains most of the terms the world of crypto comes with new terms by the second. I wish you all the best in keeping up with this ever-growing market!!! Jokes aside, there might be numerous terms out there and it depends on when you are reading this book as well. Have fun and never stop learning.

The day you stop learning is the day you stop growing!